**TEN** TRUE TALES

A Huber

# WAR HEROES
## Voices from IRAQ

### Allan Zullo

## SCHOLASTIC INC.

**New York   Toronto   London   Auckland   Sydney**

**Mexico City   New Delhi   Hong Kong   Buenos Aires**

To all the brave men and women who are serving
or have served in Iraq, especially those who have made
the ultimate sacrifice
—A.Z.

ISBN-13: 978-0-545-09026-1
ISBN-10: 0-545-09026-1

Copyright © 2009 by The Wordsellers, Inc.

12 11 10 9 8 7 6 5 4 3 2 1                    9  10  11  12  13  14/0

Printed in the U.S.A.
First Scholastic printing, January 2009

# Acknowledgments

I wish to thank the heroes featured in this book for their willingness to relive in personal interviews with me the dramatic and sometimes emotional memories of their combat experiences.

I also want to thank the following persons for their cooperation: Fred Shear, Writers Group, Office of the Secretary of Defense; Major Kirk A. Grenier, Company L, Third Battalion, Twenty-fifth Marines; Bill W. Love, Public Affairs Officer, Naval Hospital, Corpus Christi, Texas; Lieutenant Colonel D. J. Thieme, Twenty-fifth Marines; Captain Paul Greenberg, Community Relations Officer HQ, Marine Forces Reserve; Captain Erin H. Wiener, External Media Officer, Public Affairs, Marine Forces Reserve; Staff Sergeant Christina C. Delai, HQMC, Division of Public Affairs; David Altom, Kentucky National Guard Public Affairs Office; Kathy MacKnight, Naval Health Clinic New England Public Affairs Officer; Lieutenant Colonel Kevin Olson, Minnesota National Guard Director of Public Affairs; and Leigh Hutton.

Finally, a special thank-you goes to my longtime editor, Roy Wandelmaier, whose superb editing skills and publishing judgment are surpassed only by his decency and humbleness.

# Author's Note

War brings out the worst in humanity — and, ironically, the best.

The courageous members of the U.S. Army, Navy, Air Force, and Marine Corps in Iraq have risked life and limb to carry out their missions in a life-threatening world of roadside bombs, deadly ambushes, and suicidal terrorists.

Every one of these Americans is a hero.

I wish I could write all their personal stories of valor, honor, and sacrifice. But, of course, that's not possible. Instead, I set out to write a book that spotlights a few of the breathtaking acts of heroism that have happened often since this war began. First, I reviewed more than 100 military citations involving acts of bravery. Then I selected nine men and one woman who come from different branches of the military, from career Marines to army reservists. They represent some of the tens of thousands of American troops who, with steadfast courage, have been fighting a vicious enemy in a sand-blasted, war-ravaged country. And they have been willing to lay down their lives for their comrades.

All the heroes featured in the following pages earned top military medals. Some received the Navy Cross, given to a member of the U.S. Marine Corps or Navy for remarkable bravery, extraordinary heroism, and sacrifice in battle against an enemy of the United States. It is the second highest military combat honor. Several received the Silver Star, our nation's third highest combat medal, which is given to a person in any branch of the armed services who displayed exceptional courage and gallantry in action. One person earned the Distinguished Flying Cross for heroism or extraordinary achievement during combat while flying. And, for bravery, another person was awarded the Bronze Star, the fourth highest combat medal. (As of June 2008, the Medal of Honor — the nation's highest and rarest military honor — has been given to only four persons who fought in the Iraq War. They are Corporal Jason Dunham of the U.S. Marine Corps, Sergeant First Class Paul Smith of the U.S. Army, Petty Officer Second Class Michael Monsoor of the U.S. Navy, and Specialist Ross McGinnis of the U.S. Army, who were all killed in action.)

For this book, I conducted lengthy personal interviews with each one of the selected ten heroes and asked them to relive the heart-stopping moments that earned them their medals for valor. Some found it easy to talk about. Others found it difficult and emotional, because one or more of their comrades had been killed in battle. As almost any combat veteran will tell you, the most important duty of all in war is to protect the buddy on your left and the buddy on your right.

All ten persons profiled in this book shared a common trait — humility. None viewed themselves as heroes; all said they were just doing the job they were trained to do. As Sergeant Jeremiah Workman, whose bravery earned him a

Navy Cross, said, "I don't look at myself as being any different than anyone else. I did what any other Marine would have done. There are thousands of others over there [in Iraq] that deserve to be awarded, too."

Still, when you read the gripping accounts of their gutsy actions, you'll see that they displayed an intense boldness that spurred them to reach far beyond their personal limits. Some found within themselves an incredible courage that they didn't even know they had.

Their stories are written as factual and truthful versions of their recollections, although some of the dialogue has been re-created. Because there are so many military terms used in these accounts, I've included a glossary at the back of the book. Also, the complete names of a few of the heroes' comrades are not given for security reasons or because their names couldn't be verified.

Some of what you'll read is graphic. Although these passages might be hard to stomach, I have not attempted to soften them, because that is how it really happened.

Regardless of how you feel about the war in Iraq, Americans in uniform deserve our respect, our support, and our gratitude. This book is a salute to their courage, honor, and gallantry.

— Allan Zullo

# Contents

# The War on Terror

On September 11, 2001 — the day that changed the world — fanatics from the Islamic militant organization al-Qaeda struck the United States in the most devastating terrorist attack in the nation's history, killing nearly 3,000 innocent people.

In a fiendishly coordinated assault, 19 suicidal terrorists hijacked four commercial jetliners. They deliberately crashed two of the planes into New York's World Trade Center, leveling its twin 110-story towers. Another plane slammed into the Pentagon, damaging the headquarters of the U.S. Department of Defense. Before the fourth plane could reach its target — possibly the White House — it crashed into a field in Pennsylvania after passengers fought the terrorists for control of the aircraft.

Declaring a War on Terror, the United States and several allies (called coalition forces) invaded Afghanistan, because that country's government, known as the Taliban, was protecting al-Qaeda and its leader, Osama bin Laden. The American-led forces toppled the Taliban government, destroyed al-Qaeda training camps, and drove many of the organization's fighters into the rugged mountains bordering Pakistan.

Although many of al-Qaeda's top leaders were dead or captured, bin Laden managed to escape and urged terrorists around the world to attack Western countries.

In 2002, President George W. Bush accused Iraq of being a threat to the free world. He asserted that Iraq, under ruthless dictator Saddam Hussein, had links to al-Qaeda and was willing to help the terrorists' cause by giving them weapons of mass destruction. The U.N. Security Council sent inspectors into Iraq to search for such weapons, but when Iraq ignored U.N. demands for more cooperation, President Bush launched Operation Iraqi Freedom.

On March 20, 2003, the United States and its allies invaded Iraq and quickly overthrew the evil dictator, defeated his army, and dismantled his government. The invasion led to the capture and execution of Saddam Hussein, who over his brutal 24-year reign had ordered the cold-blooded killing and merciless torture of tens of thousands of his own citizens.

Ever since the invasion, the U.S. military has occupied the country and tried to establish a new democratic government in the hopes of giving the Iraqi people the freedom to chart their own future. But the process has been slow, frustrating, and violent. American forces have been battling insurgents, militants, terrorists, and ethnic groups that share a hunger for power over Iraq and a hatred of the Western world. To complicate matters, some of these fierce factions are attacking one another in a civil war there. Throughout the bloody chaos, the United States has been trying to win the hearts and minds of Iraqis by building schools and hospitals and providing some sense of security in various neighborhoods, cities, and villages.

The war has been complicated and controversial. Both military and congressional commissions have concluded that Iraq had neither weapons of mass destruction nor official ties with al-Qaeda. But because Iraq is so fragile, its government and military haven't been strong enough to quash the insurgents and create a new, safe, and free society. It has needed the help of American-led coalition forces to keep the country from fracturing even further. The continued mission of the U.S. military has come at a price: more than 4,000 American troops killed and another 30,000 seriously wounded as of March 2008, the end of the fifth year of the war.

The national debate over whether or not the invasion was necessary will be waged for many years to come. But at least there is one aspect of this war everyone can agree on: The men and women of the U.S. military have served with unbelievable courage, compassion, and commitment — and, above all, sacrifice. In this book are some of their true stories.

# "Greater Love Hath No Man..."

## SERGEANT SCOTT MONTOYA

For the Iraqi citizens in the slum now known as Sadr City, it was another tense day as the invasion of their country marked its third week. Some didn't know whether to cheer or hide from the Americans who were patrolling the dangerous and unsecured streets. They didn't know if the next block would erupt in a firefight, if the next intersection would turn into a kill zone, or if the next storefront would unleash a deadly RPG (rocket-propelled grenade). Yet, despite risking death simply by walking down the sidewalk, the people tried to carry on with their everyday lives.

On April 8, 2003, on the outskirts of the capital city of Baghdad, Sergeant Scott Montoya watched women buy vegetables at the open-air market, men tinker with cars at the auto-repair shop, and children ask soldiers for candy. The

4

33-year-old Marine scout sniper and his four-man squad had just finished delivering mail to members of another sniper team. And even though he and his men had longed for a hot meal and a hot shower after engaging in several firefights in previous days, they agreed to help another company patrol the urban area. They could have used the rest, because the biggest battle — the fight to secure Baghdad — was near.

Soon gunfire broke out a few blocks away and increased in intensity, triggering an uneasy feeling in Montoya. *We're about to get into a serious fight, and I don't feel good about this one,* he told himself. For one thing, his squad was separated from the other platoon without any mortars or tanks for support. For another, the Marines weren't sure where the small-arms fire was coming from, only that it was getting closer. Then he heard over a two-way radio that a radio operator had been shot in the head and killed by an enemy sniper.

Suddenly, rapid gunfire exploded all around him. Montoya and his men ducked behind a wall, dropped to the ground, and began shooting back. RPGs whistled overhead, and grenade blasts sent chunks of concrete into the air. Everything was happening so fast. When an RPG exploded nearby, two Marines who were crouching next to him went down. Struck by shrapnel, they suffered injuries to their heads and arms. *Five minutes into the fight and already we have casualties,* he thought.

"Corpsman!" he yelled.

A corpsman rushed over to administer first aid and then said, "We need to set up a CCP [casualty collection point]."

Rushing around the corner, Montoya and the corpsman kicked open the gate of a house that had a courtyard. "This will

5

make a good CCP," said Montoya. Then he helped escort the wounded there.

The Marines were pinned down on all sides. Another RPG smashed into a wall close to him, flinging pieces of shrapnel that tore into Montoya's forearm. But he was so focused on killing insurgents that he wasn't sure how badly wounded he was.

Through the billowing smoke of combat, Montoya and his fellow snipers were shooting at selected targets, especially Iraqi cars and pickups carrying heavily armed militants. The drivers were shot before the vehicles could reach the Marines.

But then one car did break through the Americans' line and crashed into a utility pole in the marketplace. Montoya, who was 100 yards away, saw the driver bend down. "He's got a mortar!" The sergeant sprinted close to the car and shot the militant before the man could fire his weapon. The Marines nearby cheered. Suddenly, Montoya felt a bit less overwhelmed. *The tide has turned,* he thought. *The momentum is swinging our way.*

Sergeant Scott Montoya was about to show what it means to be a Marine — but in a way that had nothing to do with killing the enemy.

The middle son of five siblings, Scott grew up in Southern California without a father figure because his dad died when the boy was young. Scott turned into a tough kid who was quick to fight and slow to forgive. Because he tended to settle any dispute with his fists, his mother took him to karate class when he was 14 in the hopes that he could channel his anger into a sport before he ended up in serious trouble.

Through martial arts, Scott discovered an untapped passion. His instructor, Paul Dye, worked patiently with the teenager and taught him to be selfless not selfish, to think of others first, and to respect authority and himself. Scott spent hours and hours learning karate and perfecting his skills until he became Dye's best and most devoted student. Scott's dedication to martial arts carried over in his daily life. As a senior in high school, he never missed a day of class and earned straight A's. By age 19, Karate Scotty was a black belt competing against adults.

After graduation, he worked as an electronics technician and martial arts instructor and attended college. When Montoya was 21, a friend told him, "I'm taking an exam for a sheriff's deputy position. Why don't you come with me and take the test, too." Montoya did. He passed; his friend failed.

After joining the Orange County sheriff's department, Montoya noticed certain deputies shared a special bond. They had their own greeting, calling one another Devil Dog and Leatherneck and saying things like "We ate the same dust." Montoya learned they were all former Marines. *They're closer within five minutes of being introduced than some of us who've known each other for years,* Montoya thought. *I want to be a part of that special brotherhood.*

He quit his job and sold his car, motorcycle, and computer. He held a garage sale to get rid of the rest of his possessions and put the money in the bank. Then he strode into the local

Marine recruiter's office and announced, "I want to be a grunt [slang for infantryman]."

"It's the hardest job in the military," the recruiter said. "You carry a pack, you stay in the field, and you're usually cold, hungry, and wet. And, oh, yeah, you're the first one to go to war."

"Sounds good to me."

"You'll also have the best training and the most exciting time of your life."

Although Montoya scored exceptionally high in his aptitude tests, which qualified him for more glamorous positions in the Corps, he insisted on being a grunt. So at the age of 25, he entered boot camp, joining recruits who were years younger than him. In fact, even his drill instructor was younger, prompting others to call Montoya Grand Old Man or Grandpa. But his age gave him an edge over the less mature "boots." He excelled at everything he did because his martial arts training had improved his discipline, mental health, physical strength, maturity, and leadership skills.

While on active duty, Montoya finished number one in the School of Infantry and spent two and a half years as the squad automatic weapons gunner on a line platoon. He shined at the rigorous and elite Scout Sniper School, where training included brutal exercises that involved beatings so he would know what to expect if he were a prisoner of war. He became an expert in escape and evasion and long-range marksmanship and was in a scout sniper platoon for 18 months. He also became a martial arts instructor and trainer.

Changing his status to that of Marine reservist, Montoya resumed his career as a sheriff's deputy. Three weeks after the devastating terrorist attacks on September 11, 2001, his reserve captain called and said, "We're probably going to war. You have forty-eight hours to decide whether you want to go back on active-duty status."

Montoya didn't hesitate. "I'm going back."

After months of more training as a scout sniper, he was shipped to Kuwait, attached to the Scout Sniper Platoon, Second Battalion, Twenty-third Marines, First Marine Division. He instructed hundreds of fellow Marines in the finer points of martial arts while they waited for orders to invade Iraq. The night before the invasion of March 20, 2003, Montoya and 1,100 other Marine grunts who would form the tip of the spear — the first to cross into Iraq — sat in the desert to hear Major General James N. Mattis say in part:

"For the mission's sake, our country's sake, and the sake of the men who carried the division's colors in past battles — who fought for life and never lost their nerve — carry out your mission and keep your honor clean. Demonstrate to the world that there is 'No better friend, no worse enemy' than a U.S. Marine."

Montoya took the words to heart. When his unit stormed across the border and charged toward Baghdad, he felt great compassion for the poor Iraqi farmers who struggled to raise their goats and herd their sheep. He tossed them packaged meals whenever he could and passed out candy to the children. But he was relentless when attacking the enemy and protecting his fellow Marines. No one was going to stop him and his men from completing their mission and routing Iraqi forces.

While waiting out a raging two-day dust storm, Montoya took a few moments to write in his journal: "I shot a man today as he popped his head out of a tower window, and he went down. I saw him shooting at the Marines behind me. It all happened so fast I am not sure what to say. His image will haunt me, and I will think about it for a lifetime. I do know that his family is sad that he is dead. . . . When men try to kill one another, only one thing becomes evident: It is better to be alive than dead.

"Being in a firefight or combat is almost like watching a videogame. Everything happens so fast, and then you have moments of clarity. . . . The smoke and the gunfire come from all directions. And the artillery is so loud that you can never get used to the explosions. . . .

"The country is riddled with war and death. . . . Wow, how the Iraqi [soldiers] have such hatred for us. If they ever capture us, they will torture and kill us. I'm not sure where all this hatred comes from, but it's very ugly. The people seem very scared of us. They mostly want food from us or smokes. The other ones want us dead. They fly red-and-black flags over their homes to show support for Saddam and his military. They also look at us, and what we're doing, and report back to their officials on the numbers and capabilities of our regimental combat team."

As the Marines pressed toward Baghdad, Montoya kept reminding himself to always do the right thing and follow his moral compass. He understood that his enemies were only those

Iraqis who chose to fight. He had no quarrel with the citizens who wanted nothing more than to raise their families and work at their jobs without fear of getting shot or blown up.

Soon he was in the middle of a ferocious firefight in Sadr City, where everything he stood for — the Marine, the trained killer, the selfless man — was being tested in ways he never could have imagined.

Across a major intersection, he saw automatic and small-arms fire coming at him from all directions. Montoya and his men met up with the other platoons in a part of the town where closed-up shops lined a normally busy thoroughfare. While the Marines were fighting Iraqi soldiers, armed militants who were crammed in cars and pickups roared by, shooting at the Americans.

"Corpsman! We need a corpsman!" a Marine yelled.

Montoya saw that a white car filled with Iraqis had been riddled with bullets and had come to a halt in the middle of the road. "They're civilians and they're hurt!" he shouted. Turning to two comrades, he urged, "Let's try to help them. It's the right thing to do."

Braving enemy fire, the trio rushed out to the car and forced open the doors. The driver, a middle-aged man, was slumped over dead with bullet wounds to the head and chest. Another man in the front seat was bleeding badly from a gaping gash in his right leg. Pointing to the hole where his shin used to be, he was crying, shaking, and jabbering in Arabic. Then he started losing consciousness.

In the backseat, Montoya saw two young women and an elderly lady who all had been shot. One of the younger women was holding her bloody stomach while the other one was clutching her hand, which had a finger blown off. The aged woman was gripping a spot on her arm that had been hit by a round. All three were hysterical. And then Montoya spotted a blood-splattered toddler huddled between them. She, fortunately, had not been hurt. "We're going to try to help you," he told the women, not sure they understood a word he said.

Gunfire from militants across the road struck near the car, driving off two of the Marines. Montoya saw that the shots were coming from a mosque 100 yards away. *I can't believe they would actually shoot at us from a holy place*, he thought.

He wanted to race for cover, but he refused to leave the civilians in the kill zone. He pointed to the street corner next to the CCP and shouted to the women, "Run over there!"

They scrambled out of the car and hustled for safety. Meanwhile, Montoya hurried around to the other side, bent over, grabbed the wounded man, and pulled him out by the shoulders. Rounds were whizzing inches over his head, so he didn't dare stand up.

Dropping to a sitting position, Montoya dragged him slowly across the road. *This is taking forever*, the leatherneck thought. *We're sitting ducks.* Seeing how exposed he was, some of his comrades kept firing at the enemy so the militants couldn't get too many clear shots at Montoya.

For 200 yards, he worked his way back with the bleeding man until they reached the CCP where the corpsman was working on the young woman who had been shot in the abdomen. She was shrieking and yelling in Arabic.

"What can I do to help?" Montoya asked.

"Stop the bleeding on the guy's leg," the corpsman replied. Montoya quickly applied a pressure bandage.

The other young woman, the one who had lost her finger, moaned over and over, "Why did you shoot us? Why did you shoot us?"

"You speak English," Montoya said with surprise. "What is your name?"

"Anna. That's my sister, Nora. I think she's dying!"

Montoya looked at the corpsman, who gave him a slight nod, indicating that he thought Nora would survive. "Doc is doing everything he can to save her."

"And our mother and my niece?"

"Your mother will be fine, and your niece wasn't harmed."

"But why did you shoot us?"

Montoya knew why. Civilians like Anna and her family were still driving on the four-lane road that sliced through the firefight, not realizing they were entering a combat zone. Some militants had lain on the ground, waiting for a civilian car to pass before shooting at the Marines. Because sound waves travel slower than bullets, it seemed to the leathernecks on the other side of the road that the occupants in the passing car were insurgents firing at them. So the Marines shot at the car, unaware that the occupants were innocent civilians.

*The Iraqis were setting us up!* Montoya thought.

More explosions rocked the block. Montoya ran toward an intersection and saw a Marine had been dazed by one of the blasts and was in shock, stumbling aimlessly about. *I've got to get him out of there*, Montoya thought.

He dashed out into the open, threw his comrade's arm over his shoulder, and brought him to safety.

In all the chaos, corpsmen had lost some of their medical gear. Bandages, wraps, pressure packs, and other equipment were scattered in the street. Trying to ignore the massive amount of bullets flying around, Montoya darted back and forth, scooping up the items and returning them to the grateful corpsmen.

The sounds of explosions from RPGs and increasing enemy firepower continued to echo off the buildings. As Montoya leaned against a wall, firing at the enemy, he spotted a fallen leatherneck, a big machine gunner, in the middle of the street. The Marine had been shot in the leg and was bleeding and unconscious. *If someone doesn't go out and get him, he'll be taken prisoner and tortured,* Montoya thought. *There's no way I can leave him there. Marines don't abandon their fellow Marines.* From his years in the Corps, he lived by an unbreakable code: As a Marine, you're never alone, because you will never be left behind just as you do not leave others behind.

Montoya scanned the area. Militants seemed to be shooting out of every open window in sight. *How am I ever going to make it to that Marine? He's pretty big, but I'm tough. My legs and back are strong.* Montoya sprinted out to the wounded leatherneck and tried to pick him up, but to his dismay, he couldn't. *He's too heavy, and I don't have the strength to carry him! I wish I was one of those superheroes right now.*

Every second Montoya remained exposed increased his chances of getting shot. *I've got to make him lighter.* It took a long minute — what seemed like an hour — for him to strip the Marine's helmet, ammunition, and machine gun and get rid of about 60 pounds of gear. *Hurry, hurry, hurry!* Montoya, wearing 80 pounds of his own equipment, finally picked up his wounded comrade, folded him over his shoulder, and plodded about 500 yards toward the CCP, fearing that at any second he would get gunned down. As shots rang out from different positions, he felt pieces of concrete thwack him in the legs from rounds that barely missed him.

*Dear God, please don't let me get hit,* he prayed. Montoya ran as best he could bent at an angle, figuring he had a better chance of living if he were shot in the rear or the back of the leg rather than in the side of his chest.

When Montoya brought the wounded Marine to the CCP, a corpsman smiled and said, "Way to go. That's number two."

*I can't believe I didn't get shot,* Montoya thought.

Returning to the battle, he soon spotted another comrade who had been wounded and was sprawled in the fire-swept street.

The enemy was shooting from several vantage points, including the mosque across the street. The Marines had orders not to shoot at a mosque, because it was a holy site. Montoya felt his humanity was being severely tested. *Do I shoot at the mosque to protect my Marine? I can't let him die out there,* he thought, staring at the prone leatherneck. *I know they're using him as bait, waiting to shoot whoever goes out to try and help him.*

Then Montoya thought of the Bible verse John 15:13, which had long been stamped in his soul: "Greater love hath no man than this, that he lay down his life for his friends." He didn't want to die, but in his heart and mind he was willing to risk his life if it meant a chance at saving another's life.

*I'll wait for a lull in the fire and then . . . boom . . . I'll run out there. I'll use the best cover, the best route, and run as fast as I can.* So once again he charged out into the open to rescue a wounded comrade. When he reached him, Montoya kneeled down, draped him over his shoulder, and then began the long run back. Despite being in top physical condition, the firefight had sapped much of his strength. Now the muscles in his legs felt like they were burning. *I can't afford to slow down.*

He didn't ask anyone to cover him. But he could tell that those Marines who saw what he was doing gave him the suppressive fire he needed. *That's what I expected they would do.* The heavy cover kept the enemy from taking aim at him.

When Montoya arrived at the CCP, the same corpsman announced, "Hey, that's number three!"

A short while later, Montoya saw another Marine go down from a grenade in the street. *How many times can I go out there before I get shot?* he wondered. Despite feeling increasingly at risk, he felt compelled to act. *While I have a breath of air in my lungs, there's no way I'm going to leave him lying there.* Montoya raced out as bullets zipped and zinged to his left and right. He threw the Marine's arm around his shoulder and together they made it to the CCP.

"Number four!" shouted the corpsman.

By now, Montoya was running out of gas. Yet, seeing another comrade staggering in the open from the effects of a nearby grenade blast, Montoya once again charged out and helped the leatherneck to safety.

"That's number five!" the awed corpsman yelled out.

The firefight lasted through the night and into the next morning. Montoya could barely function, because he was so exhausted and dehydrated. Yet he kept fighting as though his body were on automatic pilot. Incredibly, although he took some shrapnel in his arm, no bullet pierced his flesh. When the battle finally ended, the weary, drained leatherneck hurt all over. Every bone, every muscle, every organ ached.

But he felt so good in his heart. All the Marines he saved — none of whom he knew or had ever spoken to before — recovered. Later, when he summoned images in his mind of that fateful day — of the bullets, rockets, and grenades that he selflessly defied for the sake of others — he thought, *I would do it all again. Yeah, I would do it all again.*

*In 2005, Sergeant Scott Montoya received the Navy Cross for his lifesaving actions, becoming the first scout sniper of the Iraq War to earn the award. He also was given the Navy Achievement Medal for teaching martial arts to 850 Marines.*

*"There's something special about being awarded the Navy Cross by your peers, because it means they believe in you,"* Montoya said of the honor. *"What I did was an act of love. But I also want to make the distinction that it is not mine alone. I hold the Navy Cross in trust for all the Marines who came before me and those that will come after me."*

# Ambushed!

## CORPORAL JEREMIAH WORKMAN

In the fall of 2004, al-Fallujah was swarming with vicious insurgents who controlled the lawless Iraqi city. Heartless terrorists had killed four American civilians, burned their corpses, dragged them through the streets, and then hanged them from a bridge.

To drive out the enemy, thousands of U.S. Army and Marine troops attacked al-Fallujah in Operation Phantom Fury, the largest military action since the invasion of Iraq. Warplanes pounded the city with bombs before Marines moved in during a wicked rainstorm. After weeks of fierce fighting and shelling, the military divided al-Fallujah into 60 sectors, and then systematically went house to house, block by block, looking to capture or kill hiding insurgents and to uncover concealed caches of weapons.

By mid-December, the Marines had conquered most of al-Fallujah, so the battle-tested members of the Mortar Platoon, Weapons Company, Third Battalion, Fifth Marines — Dark Horse, as the battalion was nicknamed — were split in two and sent out to search houses.

On the evening of December 22, Squad Leader Corporal Jeremiah Workman and his men were relaxing at a forward operating base on the outskirts of the city, waiting to learn what sector they would be attempting to clear out the next morning. They were a tight-knit group who liked to laugh and joke during their free time.

Corporal Workman, 21, a former high school jock from Marion, Ohio, who joined the Marines fresh out of high school, was chuckling at the goofy antics of Corporal Raleigh Smith, 21, of Troy, Montana. Smith, who always kept his comrades loose, liked to act out the roles of Japanese animated heroes for laughs.

Nearby, Corporal Eric Hillenburg, 21, was penning a letter. Earlier, he had used a satellite phone from the rooftop of a building to wish his family in Indianapolis a merry Christmas. Meanwhile, Lance Corporal James R. Phillips, 21, was chatting with fellow leathernecks about his prized possession — a 1965 Ford Mustang that was being stored back home in Plant City, Florida.

The lighthearted atmosphere in their little compound changed dramatically when the other half of the platoon returned from the day's mission. Workman jumped to his feet and exclaimed, "Holy cow! You guys look like you've been in a fire!"

"Yeah, it was pretty bad out there," said a squad leader, explaining that their faces had been blackened from gunsmoke and explosives during a nasty firefight. "We were ambushed inside the second house that we entered in Sector Nineteen. Lots of grenades and a ton of rounds, but we're okay." However, three Marines from another unit who had volunteered to join the squad that day weren't so lucky. They were hurt and had to be medevaced.

Workman had a gut feeling that the next day would be a bad one for him and his men; that they, too, would be engaged in a deadly firefight. His comrades felt the same way. So they all stayed up until 2 A.M., cleaning their weapons and gear, making sure their equipment was in perfect working condition.

The next morning, the men felt relieved when they were told they were going to a different sector. But five minutes after they left the base in their Humvees, they received new orders by radio: "Go to Sector Nineteen." As soon as Workman heard the news, he felt a chill up the back of his neck.

When they reached the block of densely packed homes, he took 10 Marines to the right side of the street while his friend Sergeant Jarrett Kraft took 10 to the other side, and they began the job of clearing out insurgents. Searching the first two houses, Workman's team found some guns and ammo and carried them out to their Humvee.

Shortly after entering the third home, Workman heard a blast of machine-gunfire from the house across the street. He knew right away that Kraft and his men had run into a group of heavily armed militants. "Everybody out!" he ordered his team. "We have to help Kraft and his guys!"

As they sprinted toward the other house, they noticed gunsmoke pouring out of the second-story windows. Workman ordered several men to guard the outside to keep insurgents from fleeing and to prevent others from aiding the militants. Then he led the rest inside the enemy-infested building where he saw Kraft and another sergeant leaning against the wall of a staircase, firing up the steps while militants blazed away. Bullets were exploding so close to the Marines' heads that Workman screamed for them to get down.

He let loose with a heavy stream of suppressive fire, allowing those Marines on the ground floor to quickly exit the home. More insurgents then appeared on rooftops of neighboring houses, spraying a deadly crossover of bullets at the small American force.

"We got ambushed!" Kraft yelled to Workman. "Some of our guys are trapped upstairs!"

Moments earlier, five Marines who were clearing the house had gone into a second-story bedroom when a dozen militants jumped out of a large closet. On the other side of the room, more insurgents leaped out from behind a tall stack of blankets. Although wounded, the Marines fought their way onto a second-floor landing.

Now the enemy on the second floor was firing heavily from the open doors of three bedrooms. They had a clear shot to the staircase and were spraying the area with bullets, making communications and movement nearly impossible for the Americans. The noise was beyond deafening.

"We've got to get up there," said a lieutenant who had joined the fight. "Let's form a stack."

The men lined up behind Workman for a charge up the open stairway just inside the front door. A flash of fear swept over him. *This is a real-man check,* he told himself. *Okay, I'm a corporal in the U.S. Marine Corps and I have guys looking up to me for leadership. What am I going to do? I wish I wasn't the front man. But this is my chance to earn the respect of my fellow Marines and lead the charge up the stairs. This is what I signed up for.*

"On three, we're going up!" the lieutenant announced. "One!"

*I'm going to get shot somewhere . . .*

"Two!"

*Hopefully just in my arm or leg and not my head . . .*

"Three!"

*Oh, God, here goes nothing!* Blindly firing his M16 rifle above his head in a desperate attempt to keep the enemy from shooting at him, Workman bounded up the stairs. Enemy fire nipped at his body, yet he managed to reach a landing where a thick wall provided protection for him. *Whew, I made it! And I didn't get shot!* But when he turned around, he gasped. Nobody had followed him. He was by himself. Even though his comrades were 10 feet away, he felt as alone as if they were 10 miles away.

"Workman, get down here!" the lieutenant ordered. "We need to regroup."

"Why don't I stay and wait for you guys to get up here?"

"Get down here, now!"

Following orders, Workman closed his eyes and literally dived headfirst down the concrete steps, sliding along the stairs on his belly as bullets flew in both directions. He landed awkwardly on his collarbone at the bottom of the stairway and had the wind knocked out of him. His buddies pulled him to his feet.

"How come no one followed me up?" Workman asked.

"The guy behind you hesitated a second too long," Kraft replied.

One of the Marines then suggested, "Let's throw a grenade up there and soften them up."

"No, that's a bad idea," said Workman. "It could fall back downstairs."

Before any more discussion, someone tossed a grenade up the stairs, but just as Workman feared, it rolled back down the steps. Everyone scattered. Workman dived under the staircase a second before the grenade exploded. The blast, which chipped some of the steps but didn't damage them, flung a piece of shrapnel into the back of his leg and gave him an instant splitting headache.

"We need to get back up there and help those trapped Marines," the lieutenant said.

Once more, Workman stood at the front of the stack. *Someone needs to go first,* he told himself. *Yes, it's pretty risky. But I survived the first time without getting shot.* Although he was just as scared as before, he scrambled up the stairs, firing away. Everybody followed him, and all reached the landing safely. They crept up another set of steps to the second floor, where Workman spotted two of the trapped Marines, Jared Hebert and Raleigh Smith. One was hiding under a desk and the other was crouched next to it. Both were seriously wounded.

*They could have fled when we arrived and escaped out onto the second-floor overhang, but they didn't,* he thought. *They chose to stay and fight.* In fact, they had laid down suppressive fire, allowing Workman and the others to reach the second floor.

*Where are the other missing Marines?* Workman wondered. *Did the insurgents grab them and drag them away?*

Suddenly, a bright yellow homemade grenade rolled out of an open bedroom door. "Grenade!" he yelled to the others. *I've got three to five seconds to prepare myself for heaven.* He curled up in a ball. When it exploded, it spewed shrapnel and a huge flame that flared out into the hallway and down the staircase. The flame engulfed the Marines but didn't set them on fire. It did, however, suck the air out of their lungs for a moment and singed their eyebrows and blackened their faces.

After the flash cleared, Workman turned around and asked, "Is everyone okay?" Each of his comrades had been hit with shrapnel, but none of the wounds was serious. A piece of flying metal had slammed into his leg, making it feel as though someone had whacked him with a baseball bat.

When Workman looked toward the desk, Hebert and Smith were gone. He didn't know if they had left on their own or were taken prisoner. Despite the head-pounding bedlam and chillingly close quarters, the Marines and militants continued to trade fire. When the Americans ran low on ammo, they backed down the stairs and out of the house.

As they ran toward their Humvees to reload, Workman spotted Hebert lurching in the street. He was covered with blood from head to toe. *My God, he looks like a zombie.*

Workman scurried over to him just as insurgents began firing at them from a different house. Clutching Hebert by his flak jacket, Workman, a strapping 200 pounds, dragged his wounded smaller comrade 75 yards down the street. Bullets sent up little clouds of flying debris by their feet. Workman wanted to move faster, but couldn't, not while he was helping Hebert. Every step he took, Workman wondered if an enemy round would strike him or his comrade. None did.

They safely reached the end of the street where the Marines had set up their CCP. Those like Workman who shrugged off their minor injuries filled their empty magazines with ammo and dashed back to the house.

Although the Americans had cleared the first floor, dozens of insurgents remained barricaded in the second-floor bedrooms and were prepared to fight to the death.

Workman rallied his men and charged up the stairs to once again exchange intense gunfire with the enemy. Corporal Steve "Rambo" Snell, who was directly behind Workman, was firing an AK-47 he had found. The muzzle was only two inches from the side of Workman's head, close enough so the shell casings bounced off his neck. The noise from the weapon — firing on full automatic — was incredibly loud, throwing off Workman's equilibrium and making him dizzy.

Nevertheless, he continued to fight, tossing two grenades into a bedroom. Then other Marines handed him more grenades to throw, causing the second floor to turn dark from the smoke.

Next to him, Workman heard Lance Corporal Philip Levine groan in pain. Shrapnel from an enemy grenade had flown into

Levine's eye and knocked him down. He scrambled to his feet and then screamed in agony when an armor-piercing bullet nearly ripped his left forearm from his shoulder. What was left of his arm was charred, black, and bloody. Levine, a tough-as-nails 33-year-old veteran from the Bronx, gritted his teeth and tried to lift his rifle with his right hand but couldn't do it. So he pulled out his pistol and fired at the enemy.

"We've got to get you out of here," said Workman. He guided Levine out of the house and brought him, under heavy enemy fire, to the CCP. While Workman filled up his magazine, a corpsman gave Levine a shot of morphine and put a bandage around his arm. In terrible pain and pale from loss of blood, Levine leaned against the wall. "Give me a pistol! Just give me a pistol, and I'll go back into the house!" he shouted. But no one would let him. He was too injured.

Workman peered in the back of a Humvee and spotted Hillenburg and Smith lying on the floor. Smith had his hand over his forehead. Workman jumped into the vehicle and asked, "What happened to you?" When neither replied, he gently shook Smith. There still was no response. He put his finger on Smith's neck to feel for a pulse, but Workman was shaking so badly, he couldn't tell whether there was one. Then he leaned down and put his ear to Smith's mouth. Not hearing anything, he yelled to the corpsman, "Doc, get over here! Smith needs you!"

"It's okay," said the corpsman, who was busy tending to Hebert's wounds. "Don't worry about him."

Workman began shaking Smith. "Doc. Get over here! There's no response!"

"That's because he's dead, Corporal. He's gone."

"What about Hillenburg?"

"Leave him be, man. He's dead, too."

Then it hit Workman: *This is the Humvee where they put the dead. I've never seen a dead Marine before.* For a moment, his mind went blank and he stood still. *We just lost Marines in combat. I just lost two of my friends.* Pangs of heartache and surges of anger left him battered. He felt as though the whole world was crashing down around him. *My buddies are dead. They're really dead.* Suddenly, a wave of rage took control, and his eyes filled with vengeance.

Despite being wounded, Workman scooped up a load of magazines and began grabbing every Marine he saw. "Come on, we're going back in!" He led his team on a third assault to retrieve any remaining troops and clear the building of insurgents. Repeatedly exposed to a hail of enemy fire, Workman kept alternating his weapons — flinging grenades and firing his rifle. He cut down the enemy, two here, another there, as he helped clear one room.

The smoke was so thick it blotted out the sunlight that had been streaming through the windows. At the height of the firefight, two militants bolted from a room, shooting their weapons. Because of poor visibility, Workman couldn't see their whole bodies — just a beard or two eyes. It was as though they were ghosts floating through the dense smoke. The Marines fired round after round at them, and yet the two insurgents still managed to get back into the room. *No one could have survived our fire*, Workman thought. *Why aren't they falling over?* (He later learned that the militants were on drugs that temporarily dulled their pain, allowing them to continue shooting until they dropped dead from their fatal wounds.)

Through the heat, smoke, gunfire, and explosions, Workman fought relentlessly. But then an enemy grenade blew up, knocking him and his fellow Marines down. Like his comrades, the emotionally and physically spent Workman didn't think he could get up. *We're going to die here.*

He tried to stand, but he was too weak. Exhausted, he stumbled over to a corner of the room. He leaned against a wall and then slumped to the floor and began throwing up. He couldn't move and could barely keep his eyes open. He felt like he was looking through a straw that was getting smaller and smaller until everything went dark. *I hope all the guys got out of the house,* he told himself. *I hope they're all safe.* As he lost his vision, he thought, *I think I'm dying.* The faces of his mother and grandmother appeared in his mind, which gave him an enormous feeling of comfort. Whatever pain he had felt earlier from his battle wounds had vanished. *Yeah, I must be dying. What can be better than for a U.S. Marine to go out like this?*

But he was brought back to his senses when his battalion executive officer, Major Todd Desgrosseilliers, shook him. "Let's go," the major ordered.

"No, I want to stay here with my Marines. I want to stay until the last bullet is fired."

"Our fight is done for now. We're getting out of here."

Workman was still throwing up and too exhausted to move, so the major grasped him by the helmet and pulled him down the stairs and out of the house. Then he picked up Workman and carried him fireman-style to the street, where he poured water down the neck of the fatigued Marine. Workman slouched on the curb from the effects of dehydration. The adrenaline that had been surging through his body now overwhelmed it.

His hands trembled, his face was black from smoke, and his eyebrows were burned off. Seeing the blood seep through his cammies from his shrapnel wounds, he felt his pain increase. He checked his most severe leg wound and thought, *Thank God, I had my squad-leader notebook in my pants pocket.* The shrapnel had sliced right through it and into his thigh. *If the shrapnel hadn't been slowed down by the notebook, it would have done some major damage.*

Regaining his strength after resting briefly and guzzling water, Workman learned that a third Marine had been killed — Phillips, whose body had been recovered. The rest of the Marines were all accounted for.

Smith and Phillips had died in the house in the initial ambush. During the firefight, the insurgents had been unaware that other Marines had scrambled to the second-floor deck from an adjacent house and had carried the two bodies away by passing them man-to-man across the rooftops before lowering them to the ground. Hillenburg, meanwhile, had been killed by enemy sniper fire as he raced to assist from a block away.

At the end of the firefight, an M1A1 Abrams tank arrived with a quick-reaction force. The tank, blocking nearly the whole street, fired six rounds into the house. When Marines started getting sniper fire from atop a roof of one of the nearby homes, they quickly killed the sniper.

After calling in air power, the Americans walked two blocks away and hunkered down to watch two jets zoom low and drop their bombs. The ground shook, causing the Marines to duck while debris rained down on them. When the dust settled, Workman saw that the whole block had been leveled. To clear the area, it had taken the Marines more than 10 hours of violent fighting. The bodies of 47 militants lay dead.

The next morning, Workman, who had a corpsman pull shrapnel out of him, felt as if he had been in a major car accident. He hurt all over. But what hurt him and his fellow leathernecks the most was seeing the empty cots of Hillenburg, Smith, and Phillips. *I can't believe they're gone*, he thought. *I hope none of them suffered and that they died quickly.*

Making the day even more difficult, he and his buddies had to go through the pockets of their dead comrades' clothes and collect personal possessions to send home to the grieving families. It was the hardest task that Workman had to do during his time in Iraq. Seeing the pictures of his friends' loved ones — and knowing how much they would hurt when word of the deaths reached them — left him shaken to the core.

The three men were deeply missed. There wasn't a day that the platoon didn't think about their fallen brothers and the heartsick families.

Two weeks before leaving Iraq, Workman and his fellow Marines held a touching tribute in honor of Raleigh Smith, Eric Hillenburg, and James R. Phillips. The Marines put the boots of their fallen comrades at a 45-degree angle, stuck their weapons in the ground bayonet first, put their helmets on the butt of their rifles, and hung their dog tags on their rifles.

Later, when Workman returned to the United States, he decided to honor the three in a unique and personal way — with a tattoo. On his back is the shape of Iraq in the colors of the country's flag — red on top, white in the middle, and black at the bottom. The tattoo reads: OPERATION IRAQI FREEDOM 2, bordered on the left by 3RD BATTALION and on the right by 5TH MARINES. Below are the names of Smith, Hillenburg, and Phillips and the date he will never forget: December 23, 2004.

*Corporal Jeremiah Workman is credited with eliminating more than 20 enemy fighters during the battle. For his actions, he received the Navy Cross on May 12, 2006. The citation states that Workman "reflected great credit upon himself and upheld the highest traditions of the Marine Corps."*

*Said Workman, "I accepted this medal for three guys who didn't make it back. So it's really theirs."*

*Sergeant Jarrett Kraft also received the Navy Cross for leading his team through the deafening barrage in the house despite being hit and knocked down by shrapnel and suffering from a blast concussion. According to the citation, Kraft "demonstrated courageous leadership with a complete disregard for his own safety during this desperate two-hour battle, as he personally braved multiple enemy small-arms kill zones to render assistance and guidance to his Marines."*

# The Bomb Buster

## STAFF SERGEANT DANIEL BOGART

In Iraq, death has often lurked inside rusty tire rims, discarded shoe boxes, and old oil cans. It has reared up from rock piles, sewer grates, and trash mounds.

In the most harmless-looking things, enemy forces have hidden their deadly homemade bombs, known as improvised explosive devices, or IEDs for short. Ever since the war began, IEDs have accounted for more than half of all combat deaths and injuries of American troops.

Staff Sergeant Daniel Bogart knew all too well the devastating power of IEDs. He had seen firsthand what they can do to military vehicles, supply trucks, and fellow Marines. That's because he was a highly trained member of the U.S. Marine Corps's bomb squad, better known as the Explosive Ordnance Disposal team, or EOD. It was his job to identify, disable, and sometimes destroy these sinister makeshift bombs. Every time he encountered an IED, he knew that one false move, one simple mistake, one rushed step could kill him and countless others.

But that was a risk Bogart was willing to take. He accepted the challenge because he wanted to make a difference no matter what the danger.

During his first tour of duty in Iraq in 2004, he proved he was one of the Marine Corps's go-to guys. He had undergone rigorous training and prepared well, scoring high in written and physical-fitness exams and even on a test that measured mental toughness.

On a cold March day in 2004, Bogart's three-man team headed out on its first call in the war: A 150-vehicle convoy had been stopped on a main supply route two miles outside the city of al-Fallujah by the discovery of a roadside bomb. It was up to the Marine from Midland, Texas, to disable the IED so the convoy could complete its mission.

His team rode in a specially equipped Hummer followed by a security squad in Humvees. Packing a 9-mm pistol and slinging an M16 rifle across his chest, Bogart was weighted down by a belt that held ammo, a pouch with C-4 explosives, an igniter, and a heavy-duty knife used for digging around buried bombs. He wore a helmet and flak jacket made of a body armor fabric called Kevlar, earplugs, and special safety glasses.

Although he had trained for this moment — more than 1,100 hours of intense study and practice — Bogart was nervous when he arrived on the scene. Butterflies swirled in his stomach. He looked down the road behind him and saw all those vehicles parked, waiting to get by this menacing IED. *The pressure is on you,* he told himself. *Failure of the mission isn't an option, so don't even bother to think negatively.*

The Marines assigned to guard the EOD technicians fanned out to keep the locals away and to put the team in a protective bubble. No one got in or out without going through them.

Bogart brought out the fourth member of the team from his vehicle, a three-foot-tall, occasionally reliable robot with antennae, spindly arms, and treads like those on army tanks. In the backseat of his vehicle, Bogart settled in front of a small monitor and started yanking at a pair of joysticks, maneuvering the robot toward the IED.

He saw on the screen that the bomb was a huge South African–made 155-mm artillery shell connected to a remote detonator with a long-range cordless telephone base station (the unit or stand that cradles the handset). The robot found a wire that led to an antenna under the ground. Bogart brought the robot back, put an explosive charge in its claw, and then maneuvered it over to the phone's base station. The robot placed the charge and then returned to the vehicle. The explosive charge destroyed the base station without setting off the artillery shell. Without the base station, the terrorist would be unable to use his or her phone to set off the IED.

After the IED was disabled, it was moved to a safe area in the middle of a nearby field and blown up. Bogart collected the separated components such as the base station, battery, wires, and other fragments. Then he sent them off to analysts to examine for fingerprints, hair, saliva, and other possible trace evidence. They hoped to find clues that would lead them to the perpetrators or the source of the IED. Ultimately, their findings would end up at the FBI's data center in the United States.

When that section of the road was secured, the trucks in the convoy revved up their engines and continued on their way. Watching 150 vehicles roar past — loaded with troops and supplies — Bogart felt a surge of pride and satisfaction. *This is what I want to do,* he thought. *This is definitely a worthwhile job.*

At the start of the war, insurgents in Iraq fashioned IEDs from whatever they could find. Limited only by their own imaginations, the bomb makers used timers from everyday items such as washing machines or tied artillery shells to motorcycle batteries and cordless phones. Soon car-door openers, short-range radios, and cell phones replaced simpler remote-controlled triggers, allowing the terrorists to move farther and farther away from the IEDs before setting them off. But the U.S. military countered with sophisticated radio-frequency jammers that often thwarted bomb triggers.

Insurgents began swapping tactics on Web sites, and whenever American forces caught on, the terrorists moved to newer methods. IEDs became more complex. And when the enemy started targeting EOD teams while they were trying to defuse the bombs, the military answered with a legion of advanced robots and more security forces.

For Bogart and other EOD personnel, it was like playing a deadly game of chess. In the battle of wits and technology between insurgents and bomb-disabling squads, the winners were the ones who adapted the fastest, reacted the quickest, and improvised the best. Bogart seldom saw the same kind of IED twice. He and his team constantly changed their procedures because they knew the enemy was watching their every step and trying to outsmart them.

Bogart and his EOD squad were like firefighters, ready to respond on a moment's notice. Some days, they had no calls. Other times, they had as many as 13, one after the other, that kept them busy for up to 30 straight hours without much of a break.

Every call was different. Every call was perilous. Some days, he felt more uneasy than on other days. But he always stayed focused and refused to let fear overtake him. On a few occasions, he had to put on an 80-pound, olive green Kevlar protective suit that made him look like a dressed-up sumo wrestler. Other times he had to disable a bomb while under small-arms fire and mortar attacks.

It was up to his security force to give him the protection he needed to get the job done. Time and again when he had to defuse an IED by hand, there would be the following conversation:

"Everyone stay back," he says.

A member of the security force responds, "We're coming with you."

Bogart shakes his head. "I'm going down there hands-on. I'll be three feet away from the IED. Don't follow me. Just cover me."

"No, we're going with you," the Marine insists. "We're here to protect you. You're not going down there alone."

"Look, I won't even take my guys with me, because it's too dangerous. I'm not taking you with me."

"It's not your choice. We're going to protect you."

Bogart takes a deep breath and begins creeping toward the IED. He hears more than one pair of boots crunching the ground right behind him. *They won't let me go alone,* he thinks. *That's way beyond what they're required to do. They don't have to do that — but I'm glad they're looking out for me.*

Whenever Bogart inched up to an IED, he tried to analyze the electrical circuit in the deadly device to determine its path. He needed to find a way to disrupt that circuit without accidentally dumping a charge into the blasting cap, which would set off the bomb.

Even after he successfully disabled an IED, he often faced other dangers. One day in September 2006, during his second tour, Bogart and his team had finished a call involving an intricate IED that he had disarmed. The members were feeling good about their accomplishment as they drove back toward the base with two security vehicles in front of them. The EOD team was riding in a Cougar, a heavily armored truck designed to withstand roadside bombs.

Suddenly, to their stunned amazement, a section of the entire road flew up and over them as if sucked off the ground by a fierce tornado. Then came a thunderous roar. They had been struck by an explosion so powerful that it lifted their 24-foot-long, 26-ton vehicle off the ground. The Cougar (which weighs about twice the average school bus) crashed into the crater left by the blast, but then drove through the smoke and debris and back on the road. No one said a word at first. All Bogart heard were shrapnel from the bomb and fragments from the road pelting the vehicle, which suffered little damage.

Fortunately, none of the leathernecks was hurt. The bomber apparently was so excited about the opportunity to blow up some Americans that he set off the IED just a few seconds too early and missed the Cougar by about 10 feet. "He didn't get us, but he sure got my attention," Bogart joked with his team. It was one of 10 attempts on his life during his time in Iraq.

As in all wars, life and death is often a matter of good fortune or bad luck. One time, Bogart and his team pulled up to an intersection to disable an IED. Arriving with them were four vehicles loaded with Marines who formed a protective bubble around the EOD guys.

While Bogart began to examine the bomb, one of the Marines walked to the corner of a nearby building. He trained his weapon down the street to stop anyone from coming close. Seconds later, a hidden bomb exploded directly underneath him.

Bogart looked up and couldn't believe his eyes. The Marine flew 60 yards (more than half a football field long) over the top of the military vehicles and landed on the other side of the road — on his feet! Turning to his amazed comrades, the Marine shouted, "Oh, my God! That was so cool!" Then he hustled back to the corner and resumed his post. Incredibly, there wasn't a scratch on him. The only discomfort he felt was a bad bruise on his heel.

Like everyone else around him, Bogart was astonished at what he had just witnessed — a one-in-a-million experience. Normally, a bomb like that would have killed or seriously injured the leatherneck. Somehow, though, he stood in exactly the right position to ride the explosion's blast wave, which thrust outward at a faster force than the deadly shrapnel that followed, so he wasn't hurt.

Not long after that extraordinary incident, Bogart saw another example of how fickle fate can be. A fellow Marine was three quarters of a mile from an IED that had detonated, far enough from the blast that he didn't pay any attention to it. Yet, a piece of shrapnel the size of a pebble traveled that entire distance and hit him in the hip. Tragically, it ricocheted off his hip bone, severed both of his lungs, lodged in his heart, and killed him instantly.

Times like those left Bogart lying awake at nights, wondering if he would make it home alive to see his wife, Melissa, and grade-school kids, Kimberly and Austin. For good luck, he kept in his wallet pictures of his children, a two-dollar bill that his father had sent him, and a four-leaf clover laminated in plastic with the words LUCK OF THE IRISH that his mother got for him during a trip to Ireland.

Bogart wasn't carrying his billfold on the evening of October 29, 2006, when he was part of a route-clearing mission that involved the EOD team, army engineers, and combat engineers. They were in a convoy of 13 vehicles — 5 Humvees and 8 specially equipped trucks, including 2 Cougars and a Buffalo, a blast-resistant truck with a mechanical arm that can dig up buried IEDs. The lead vehicle was a Husky, a small tractor equipped with a metal detector on the bottom that can pin-point buried bombs, weapons, and ammunition. The job of Bogart's team was to clear the road and intersections of IEDs so that the combat engineers could safely come in and blow up each intersection, rendering it unusable by insurgents.

Their work, which began at 5 P.M., dragged on through the night — which was interrupted by a nasty firefight — and continued into the next morning without a break.

Near one of the targeted intersections, the Husky was struck by an IED. The explosion blew the front tires off the vehicle but did little other damage and didn't hurt anyone. While the Marines put on new tires, Bogart did a post-blast analysis of the bomb, and then the group continued toward the next intersection.

On its way, the convoy was attacked by four insurgents firing AK-47s. It took security forces about 10 minutes to fend them off before the Americans pushed on.

As the convoy neared a muddy intersection, a Marine in the lead vehicle spotted an IED. But Bogart had no means of inspecting the bomb remotely. The hydraulic lines on his vehicle had been damaged either by the firefight or the IED attack. The Buffalo's robotic arm failed to unearth the IED, and the muddy conditions prevented him from using the robot, which because of recent glitches wasn't working properly.

"I'll have to do this by hand," Bogart told his comrades. Doing it by hand was his last resort. As he stepped out of the vehicle, he kept in mind that the enemy often hid two or three other IEDs close to the one that was easily spotted. The insurgents figured they had a better chance of killing someone from a hidden bomb no matter which direction the person or vehicle approached from.

Bogart kept his focus on the IED and any other possible ones hidden nearby. He moved quickly but deliberately. Staying in a crouched position, he constantly scanned the ground, his eyes sweeping back and forth, searching for anything suspicious along the road, especially for command wires or firing devices that could set off the bomb. *Looking, looking, looking . . . What's that? Just a rock . . . Looking, looking . . .* His eyes studied every divot and every tire track in the road.

When he reached the IED, he saw a wire leading to a pair of pressure plates. Carefully, he snipped the wire so the bomb couldn't detonate. *Okay, that's one. But there's probably more here. If the enemy is watching, they know I've dismantled it. Are they going to start shooting? Can't think about that. If bullets fly, just hit the ground and let the security guys handle it. Okay, where's the next one?* He started walking back toward his vehicle while searching for more IEDs.

"Hey, over here!" shouted a Marine. "I've found another one!"

Bogart called over his partner, Tony (whose last name is withheld for security reasons), and together they disarmed the second one. The muddy conditions were making it nearly impossible to dig it out of the ground. They continued to examine the area and within minutes found a third hidden IED.

Because the convoy had to be on the other side of the intersection to avoid being blown up, the trucks began moving past Bogart and Tony, who were standing a few feet away from the third IED. For an unknown reason, the eleventh vehicle in the group didn't follow in the same tracks as the others. Instead, it rumbled toward the two EOD guys.

Suddenly, a tremendous blast lifted Bogart off the ground. He was tossed in a whirlwind of flying muck and debris and then slammed down hard into the mud face-first. For the next few seconds, everything was silent, except for a harsh ringing in his ears. Although dazed, he knew instantly that the vehicle had struck a fourth buried IED.

When he looked up, Bogart saw the busted tire of the vehicle only inches from his head. The hood and headlights had been ripped off by the explosion, and pieces of the vehicle were lying next to him in a crater. Shaking and woozy, Bogart slowly rose to his knees. He noticed that fellow Marines seemed to be yelling at him, but he couldn't hear a thing. That's when he realized that the blast had damaged both his eardrums.

As he staggered to his feet, he spotted Tony lying in another crater off to the side a few feet away. Tony was in an awkward position with his legs behind him, and his face and right arm were bleeding badly.

Marines were running from their vehicles to help the two men. Despite his condition, Bogart had the presence of mind to warn them to stay back. He had worked scenes before where Marines got hurt from an IED only to have comrades rush in and get injured from yet another bomb. He knew the cardinal rule: *If one of us is hurt, one of us needs to get the other out, because we're the only ones equipped to handle the situation in case of another IED.* His training and practice took over.

Clearing his head, Bogart shouted, "Stop! Don't move. Don't come any closer! There's another IED here! And there could be more of them hidden nearby, so move back."

"But you're hurt, and so is Tony," said one of his comrades.

"I know," replied Bogart, who could now barely hear. "But I don't want anyone to come in and get hurt, too. Let me handle this."

Bogart wobbled over to Tony, who couldn't open his eyes because he had taken shrapnel to his face. One of the fragments had lodged through his eyelid and into his eye socket. His right arm was covered in blood. Tony could talk, but he and Bogart were having trouble communicating with each other because of their hearing problems.

Through hand signals, Bogart kept his comrades away while he scoped the ground again. Once he felt convinced the area was safe, he guided Tony to the nearest vehicle, where a corpsman immediately began treating Tony, who remained calm but was worried about his injuries.

Bogart was injured, too, from shrapnel, but he refused any on-site treatment. Ignoring the pain and discomfort from his wounds, he went back to the intersection and disarmed the third IED. Still trying to shake off the effects of the explosion, he recovered equipment that had been scattered from the blast of the fourth IED.

Only then did he agree to return to the base with Tony for further medical care. Bogart was so focused on his job that he hadn't realized how hurt he was. On the ride back, he thought he was sweating and wiped his brow with his shirtsleeves. When he looked at his sleeves, he was surprised to see they were wet with his own blood. He had suffered injuries to his face and head.

During the 45-minute ride back to the base, the corpsman was busy treating Tony because he was in much worse shape than Bogart. In addition to wounds to the face, Tony's right arm had been severely peppered by shrapnel. The corpsman stemmed the bleeding and prevented Tony from going into shock. Bogart, meanwhile, kept talking to his partner, trying to reassure him. "You're going to be all right, Tony."

"But I can't see."

"Don't worry about that right now. Just hold on until we get you to the hospital."

Tony suffered 160 fragmentation wounds, about half to his face, including the piece of shrapnel that had damaged his eye. But surgery saved his sight and right arm, and he made a full recovery.

At the base, doctors removed 17 pieces of shrapnel from Bogart's face. Another piece had badly bruised his leg. *Man, am I lucky,* he thought. *My injuries are only superficial. It's a shame Tony got the worst of it.*

Because his hearing was greatly impaired, Bogart couldn't talk to his wife, Melissa, on the phone to tell her he was okay. So he had another member of the team call Bogart's best friend back in the United States and explain what happened. The friend then went to Melissa's house to break the news in person. Once Bogart knew that Melissa had been informed, he followed up with a detailed e-mail to her.

He took the next 12 days off to recuperate. He could have told the military, "I've had enough. I'm tired, I'm injured, and

I'm going home." No one would have had any hard feelings if he had left. But Bogart was the team leader, and it was his duty to stay there. *As long as my guys are here, I need to be here,* he told himself.

Although he wasn't superstitious, he realized that he had never been hurt whenever he had carried the photos of his kids, the lucky two-dollar bill, and the four-leaf clover with him. So when he returned to duty, he made sure to take his billfold with him. He was never going to leave it behind again.

*Staff Sergeant Daniel Bogart participated in 174 combat missions during his seven-month deployment in Iraq in 2006 and 2007 as the team leader of the First Explosive Ordnance Disposal Platoon, First Marine Logistics Group. He disposed of more than 11,000 pounds of unexploded ordnance and personally neutralized 65 IEDs, saving countless military personnel from harm.*

*In 2007, Bogart received the Bronze Star with Valor and his Senior EOD insignia in recognition of his courage and expertise. Bogart's decorations also include a Purple Heart and the Combat Action Ribbon.*

*He was quick to credit his comrades-in-arms for his many successful missions. "It is easy to do good things when you are set up for success, surrounded by the best individuals, and a good chain of command," he said. "I could not have done anything on my own. It was a team effort."*

# Do or Die

## SPECIALIST JASON MIKE

Just minutes into a brutal ambush, terrorists were shooting at Specialist Jason Mike and inching closer to his parked Humvee from opposite directions. The odds were stacked against him, because already two of his three comrades were too wounded to fight. Then his gunner — the soldier who was manning the .50-caliber machine gun atop their vehicle and keeping the enemy at bay — got shot in the hand. Without the gunner, Mike knew they would soon be overrun and then captured, tortured, and killed.

Mike had to buy time until his gunner could treat himself and get back on the .50-cal. Somehow Mike had to fend off the terrorists who were approaching from his left and right. *What did we get ourselves into?* he thought. There was only one way out of this deadly dilemma. *This has to work, or else. . . .*

Jason Mike was an army brat whose father spent 20 years in the military. After the family settled in Fort Knox, Kentucky, Mike set his sights on playing football rather than following in his dad's footsteps. At five feet nine inches tall and weighing 250 pounds, Mike was a fullback for Jacksonville (Florida) University. He had dreams of one day turning pro.

But the terrorist attacks of September 11, 2001, changed all that. While on the team plane to a game a month later in New York, Mike saw from the air the still-smoking remains of the collapsed World Trade Center's twin towers. The grim sight tore at his heart. He felt an even stronger anguish when he visited Ground Zero. It was at that moment he knew he had a greater calling: *I'm going to hang up my football cleats and put on combat boots.*

He decided to become a medic in the U.S. Army National Guard in part because of his football background. As he explained to his family, "Fullback isn't a glorified position. You block for the running back or you help protect the quarterback. You sometimes get the ball on third and one. But you know you can be a difference-maker by making that block or getting that first down. By being a medic, I feel I can be a difference-maker in combat. I can be one of those guys on the team who doesn't get the glory. But when it comes down to a crucial play, when it's fourth and one, the team needs him on the field. In much the same way, if someone is shot in a battle, they need the guy who can go out there and bandage him up."

Mike figured he would end up in Afghanistan, where the leaders of the terrorist organization responsible for the

9/11 attacks were holed up. But more than three years after the attacks, Mike, then 24, was deployed to Iraq, attached to the 617th Military Police Company of the Kentucky Army National Guard.

He joined a 10-person squad of guardsmen from different backgrounds and races: Mike, the son of an African-American father and Korean mother; Sergeant Joe Rivera, the son of a Puerto Rican father and Korean mother who was a friend of Mike's mom; Specialist Jesse Ordúñez, a Mexican-American; female soldiers Sergeant Leigh Ann Hester and Specialist Ashley Pullen; Specialists Casey Cooper, Bryan Mack, and William Haynes; Sergeant Dustin Morris; and their Kentucky-bred squad leader, Staff Sergeant Timothy Nein, 33, whose ancestors had fought in every American war since the Revolution in 1776. In civilian life, the squad was made up of a shoe-store manager, housewife, hotel manager, printer, college students, and office workers.

Despite their diversity — or because of it — they jelled as a hardworking, close-knit team and performed their duties with diligence and tenacity. In Iraq, they patrolled up and down 25-mile sections of highway south of Baghdad for months, looking for ambush sites and roadside bombs. Their main job was to follow behind supply-truck convoys that entered their sector and protect the vehicles and drivers from attacks.

Nein insisted his team study the routes, maps, and terrain for every mission. After each trip, he reviewed with his troops what they did right, what went wrong, and how they could do better. They reconned the area so thoroughly that they knew the locations of all the side roads, canals, ditches, and terrorists' escape routes. Because the squad members tried to think like the enemy and anticipate ambushes, they developed plans for every possibility in case of an attack. During their first few months in country, they faced their share of highway ambushes — and repelled every one of them.

Mike and his comrades did thorough maintenance checks after each attack. The MPs made sure to store arms, ammunition, medical supplies, and equipment in the same place and same way in each of their three armored Humvees. That way, if one of the soldiers ended up in another vehicle during a firefight, he or she knew where everything was. No group was better prepared than the members of the Second Squad of the 617th.

While on routine patrol on March 17, 2005, the squad took its turn for a break just as a convoy rolled into their sector. The MPs drove 15 miles to refuel, stretch their legs, and grab a bite to eat. But their break was interrupted when they heard over their radios that the convoy had been ambushed at the spot where the MPs had been minutes earlier. The squad jumped into the vehicles and raced to the scene, but it was too late. Out of 30 trucks in the convoy, 16 had been shot up and 4 drivers killed.

Seeing the death and destruction, the squad members agreed that on their next mission, they would not take a single break, nor stop for any reason other than to pee. Before going out on patrol on Palm Sunday, March 20, Nein told the squad, "We're going to go all-out, hit this road hard, and make sure nothing happens."

Like his comrades, Mike triple-checked his equipment and medical supplies, making sure everything was ready. Although they had never talked about it before, he and the three soldiers he rode with came up with a new plan in case they needed more firepower during an ambush: The gunner, William Haynes, who manned the Humvee's .50-caliber machine gun, would toss his other weapon, an M249 light machine gun, to the driver, Bryan Mack. Mack would then give his M4 carbine assault rifle to Mike, who otherwise carried only a 9-mm pistol.

Nein was in the lead Humvee with driver Dustin Morris and gunner Casey Cooper. One hundred and fifty yards behind in the second Humvee rode Leigh Ann Hester, Ashley Pullen, and Jesse Ordúñez. Mike and his three comrades were in the trailing Humvee. Using the call sign *Raven 42*, the squad began providing security for 30 civilian tractor trailers near the village of Salman Pak, southeast of Baghdad. The trucks were moving supplies along a four-lane highway where terrorists in small groups of 10 to 15 had been launching hit-and-run attacks in previous weeks.

The MPs were shadowing the half-mile-long convoy, staying back about 500 yards so any terrorists in the area wouldn't realize that the squad was in the rear, ready to react to any assault. Late in the morning, a semi near the front of the line swerved right, then left. Trucks began braking erratically.

"They're taking fire!" shouted Cooper from the gunner's hatch in Nein's Humvee.

Normally, a convoy is supposed to push through any ambush and keep driving to get out of the kill zone. But the enemy played this attack smart. They disabled the lead truck, creating a bottleneck. The convoy couldn't ram through, and as a result, the trucks stuck in the middle were getting blasted by RPGs and mortars in the kill zone.

"Go! Go! Go!" Nein ordered his squad over the radio. "We're going to push forward!" The other two MP vehicles followed his Humvee as they cut over into the opposite traffic lane and sped toward the front of the convoy.

In the backseat of the last Humvee, Mike could hear gunfire from AK-47s and explosions. "The trucks are getting hit bad," Haynes yelled down from his gunner's position.

Mike felt an adrenaline rush, much like he did when he ran out onto the football field at Jacksonville University. He was pumped and looked forward to quashing the ambush, because the squad had always succeeded. *This should be no different than before,* he thought. *There're probably 10 insurgents. We'll have fire superiority, and we'll move faster and smarter than they will.* He figured it would be like soldiers with guns fighting an enemy that had only knives. *This will be over in about two or three minutes.*

Zooming up the oncoming traffic lane, the three Humvees wheeled through an opening between two flaming trucks that had been struck by RPGs. The squad emerged between the convoy and the terrorists — right in the middle of the kill zone where gunfire was the heaviest. Suddenly, the enemy shifted its focus from destroying the supply trucks to attacking the MPs.

Insurgents, many wearing masks and civilian clothes, fired AK-47s, RPGs, and RPK machine guns from behind trees and mounds of dirt in a nearby orchard. The Humvees were getting pounded by rounds while the gunners of all three vehicles fired back. Mike stared at the door, wondering if the enemy bullets that were striking his vehicle would pierce all the way through and hit him.

Mike's hand went to his pocket, where he kept a tiny one-ounce bottle of prayer oil that had been blessed by his church. The devout Pentecostal Christian always carried it with him because it brought him comfort. *Gee, there're an awful lot of muzzle flashes out there*, he thought.

Just ahead was a paved side road. "Flank 'em down the road!" ordered Nein, who figured it would be the best way to cut off the terrorists — which he estimated, at first, to be no more than 10 — from fleeing.

In the lead Humvee, Morris accelerated to make the turn, when Cooper, who was exposed in the vehicle's turret, shouted, "RPG!" The projectile exploded above the rear-passenger's window, causing the Humvee to fishtail. Cooper dropped with a thud into the cab. Nein reached back, shook him, and said, "Coop, are you okay?"

Cooper didn't move.

"I think he's dead!" Nein told Morris. "I'm going to get up on the weapon."

As Nein scrambled over Cooper, the gunner came to and mumbled, "I'm okay, I'm okay. I just had my bell rung." Shaking the cobwebs out of his head, Cooper climbed back into the turret and began firing his .50-cal.

Despite the hit, the Humvee was still running. When it turned onto the side road, bullets battered the grill, causing oil to spurt onto the windshield. Morris flipped on the wipers, smearing oil over the thick glass, and stopped about 200 yards down the road. The second Humvee — with Pullen driving, Hester in the passenger seat, and Ordúñez on top with an MK19 grenade launcher and M240B machine gun — halted about 50 yards behind.

The third Humvee made the turn and stopped just beyond the corner. From the gun turret above Mike, Haynes laid down a massive amount of .50-cal fire. Hearing how much he was firing, Mike wondered, *Is there a bigger enemy force than I think?*

"There're a lot of 'em out here!" Haynes shouted. "A lot of 'em!"

Mike looked out the window. What he saw stunned him. About 16 to 20 insurgents lined a trench parallel to the main road. Another dozen or so were firing from an orchard. Still more lined a trench that ran parallel to the side road. *Oh, oh. We're way outnumbered — more than three to one,* he thought. *I didn't expect to be fighting a force this huge.* The ambush was far larger than any the MPs had ever faced. And Mike's Humvee was parked in the most dangerous spot of all — in the line of fire of the insurgents shooting from the main trench.

Mack and Rivera jumped out of the Humvee and fired back. *Things are going bad,* Mike thought. *It's game time, time for me to soldier up and do what I was trained to do.* He charged out of the vehicle as smoke churned, dust swirled, and dirt spewed. Using the Humvee for cover, he fired his 9-mm pistol. *We've got to knock these guys out.* The insurgents in the trench were pushing toward the Americans' position while enemy gunfire came from other directions as well.

Mike's pistol wasn't effective, so he called a switch. He grabbed Mack's M4 carbine while Mack manned the M249. Now Mike felt he was in a better position to help turn back the assault.

"Aw!" screamed Mack. "I'm hit!" Grasping his left shoulder, he slumped behind the Humvee.

Mike rushed over to him and said, "How can you be hit? We're behind the truck. There shouldn't be anyone behind us." He turned around and saw a muzzle flash coming from a 10-foot berm on the other side of the Humvees. Enemy bullets were flying from two directions now — the left and right side of the vehicles.

Grimacing in pain, Mack could no longer shoot and was having difficulty breathing. Mike ushered him into the back of the Humvee and bandaged him up enough to slow down the bleeding. "The bullet has lodged in your lung," Mike said. "Stay inside." Mike kept the door open so he could monitor Mack's condition. Every time Mike heard Mack scream out, the medic knew that his comrade was still alive and getting enough oxygen.

Mike squeezed off several more rounds downrange when Joe Rivera yelped and collapsed. The medic scrambled over to him. A bullet had entered Rivera's lower back, nicked his spine, and exited through his stomach. "I can't move my legs," Rivera moaned. "I think I'm paralyzed from the waist down." But he was still trying to fire back while enemy rounds were striking the ground only inches from his head.

Knowing that Rivera was too exposed to enemy fire, Mike dragged him to the back of the vehicle, but couldn't get him inside, because Rivera couldn't stand up.

*I can't leave him outside,* thought Mike. *He'll get shot. And I can't treat him out here, or we'll both get shot.* "Joe, I'll get you help, but right now this is the best I can do for you." The medic then shoved him under the Humvee for protection. "I'm sorry I don't have time to treat you right now, Joe," Mike said as he began firing more rounds downrange. "It's just that they're so many of them. . . ."

"I understand," Rivera said. "Just calm down. You'll shoot better that way. Jason, we're going to win this." Rivera's words helped Mike keep his emotions in check and concentrate on killing the enemy.

But then Mike heard another shout of anguish. This time it was Haynes, who had his machine gun trained on the insurgents in the main trench. He fell from the turret and into the Humvee, yelling, "I've been hit!"

"Where?" asked Mike.

Haynes held up his left hand. It was a mangled bloody mess.

"I know you're hurt, but your gun is our key to surviving this firefight," Mike said.

"I can stay on the gun, Jason. Just fix me up."

"If I do that, then there won't be anyone firing at the enemy. They'll overrun us for sure." Mike picked up a bandage and tossed it to him. "Wrap up your hand while I try to buy us some time until you can get back to your gun."

*Three of my guys are wounded within minutes of one another,* thought Mike. *I guess I'm next. Well, if it happens, I'm going down fighting.*

He grabbed the M249 light machine gun and propped it up

on the back of the Humvee. With his right hand on the trigger, he laid down fire in the trench line, spraying bullets back and forth. With his left hand, he fired the M4 carbine assault rifle in the opposite direction, pouring rounds in the direction of the insurgent who had shot his comrades from behind. Mike had never fired a weapon with his left hand, let alone two weapons at the same time.

But there was no other way. He had to put down suppressive fire in both directions simultaneously so the enemy couldn't advance from the front or the back. He valiantly held off the insurgents long enough in front and behind until he heard Haynes back on the gun. The reverberating sound of the .50-cal spewing lead was music to the medic's ears. Seeing the militant who had been firing at them from behind, Mike clasped both hands on the carbine and raked him with bullets. The gunman toppled over backward.

Mike then radioed for help. "I have three guys who are hit," he told Ashley Pullen, who was in the second vehicle. "I need some backup. I need help before Rivera bleeds out."

Pullen and gunner Jesse Ordúñez drove through a blizzard of bullets to the third Humvee's position. Pullen backed up her vehicle and parked it parallel to Mike's Humvee and then pulled Rivera out from under it so that he was between the two. With Ordúñez covering her, Pullen carried out instructions from Mike, who was still firing his assault rifle. Each vehicle had a combat lifesaver (CLS) bag, which consisted of IV solution, bandages, and other items needed for basic first aid. She placed a bandage over the wound and applied pressure. "Prep an IV bag for me so I can get a line into him," Mike told her.

Rivera's pain increased with each passing minute. Lying on his back, he rocked back and forth. "I can't feel my legs. What a nightmare!"

"Think about your son," said Pullen. "Think about him or anything else but this."

While following directions from Mike, who continued to shoot at the enemy, Pullen worked feverishly to stabilize Rivera. Mike glanced over at her and saw dirt kicking up behind her. *I thought she had perfect cover,* he thought. That's when he noticed muzzle flashes flaring from an open window of a farmhouse about 300 yards away. *It's a sniper, and he's getting a real good bead on Pullen. I've got to take him out or else I'll have a fourth casualty on my hands.*

Mike called up to Haynes and, referring to an antitank rocket launcher, said, "Give me the AT-Four!"

Haynes handed him the weapon, which has a maximum effective range of 300 yards — the exact distance to the farmhouse. Mike needed to make a perfect shot. The only drawback was that he had never fired one before in combat. *I can do this,* he told himself. He engaged the rocket launcher, aimed, and pulled the trigger.

Mike watched with anticipation as the projectile shot out and headed directly toward the farmhouse. It slammed into the structure and exploded, sending up debris, flames, and smoke. He had killed the sniper. Mike was so thrilled that he shouted, "I hit it! I hit it!" Pumping his fist in the air, he yelled to Ordúñez, "Did you see that? Wasn't that amazing?"

Ordúñez, who never took his eyes off the enemy and was still firing his .50-cal, said, "Hey, Jason, quit celebrating. We're still getting shot at."

Minutes earlier, at the start of the firefight, the squad members in the first two Humvees also feared they might get overrun. Nein figured their best chance was to go on the offensive and charge the attackers. Instead of dismounting on the driver's side — away from the shooting — he opened the door and ran directly toward the gunfire, killing a militant who wielded an RPG.

While Cooper and Ordúñez were showering the orchard with rounds from their machine guns, Pullen alternated between firing her weapon from behind her vehicle and manning the radio.

Morris and Hester joined Nein in an effort to silence the heaviest enemy fire, which was coming from the terrorists' trench. By shuttling forward in 10-yard rushes, the three reached the enemy's position. Hester launched two grenades and provided cover fire for Nein, who tossed more grenades. As Nein, Hester, and Morris plowed ahead, the battle turned decisively in the MPs' favor.

Hester followed Nein when they rolled into the trench. Hugging the side, they crept about a foot apart while bullets thumped in the dirt around them. The five-foot four-inch Hester, 23, shot over the shoulder of the lanky 36-year-old squad leader. Her barrel was so close to Nein's head that he felt the percussion of each shot slap his cheek. Together the two of them killed the insurgents who had stayed in the trench to fight to the death.

When Hester and Nein climbed out of the trench, 27 bodies littered the area. The only sounds were the moans and wails of six wounded terrorists. Another militant was captured hiding in the field, pretending he was dead.

Nein examined the seven cars that the insurgents had planned to use for their escape. The doors and trunks were open. The enemy apparently had planned to take hostages, because the MPs found some of the terrorists were carrying handcuffs.

The convoy had taken a beating. Several trucks were damaged beyond repair, and three civilian drivers were killed.

Mike and Pullen helped transport the wounded to a makeshift landing zone for evacuation by helicopters two miles away. Mike's biggest concern was Mack, because the round had gone through his shoulder and pierced his lung. Mack's airway was damaged, so the medic focused on him. Although Rivera was seriously wounded, his vital signs showed he was stable, and his bleeding was under control.

Knowing that Haynes and Mack were friends since their kindergarten days in Paducah, Kentucky, Mike put the two next to each other so Haynes could encourage Mack while Mike treated him.

Once the enemy weapons were secured and the MPs had picked up the militants' unused grenades, Mike began treating the wounded insurgents — the same ones who minutes earlier were shooting at him. He arranged for them to be medevaced, too.

Although emotionally it wasn't easy, he felt a duty to give them the same care he would give his own soldiers. As they called out Allah's name, he reminded himself, *They're human beings and not just the enemy.*

Later that night back at the base, Mike was lying in bed when he thought about how difficult it had been to treat the insurgents. *We Americans are the bigger persons when it comes to helping our wounded enemies. If the situation were reversed, they would have kidnapped us and tortured us. That shows how much we play by the rules of warfare. I'm sure glad to be an American.*

*For their heroic actions during that ambush, eight members of the squad received medals in 2005. Specialist Jason Mike was awarded the Silver Star for valor in battle. Also earning the medal was Sergeant Leigh Ann Hester, who became the first woman to receive such an award since World War II. Staff Sergeant Timothy Nein earned a Silver Star, too, but it was upgraded in 2006 to the Distinguished Service Cross, second only to the Medal of Honor for army personnel.*

*Specialists Casey Cooper, William Haynes, and Ashley Pullen each received a Bronze Star with Valor. Sergeant Dustin Morris and Specialist Jesse Ordúñez were each given an Army Commendation Medal with Valor.*

*Haynes, Specialist Bryan Mack, and Sergeant Joe Rivera recovered from their injuries, thanks, in large part, to Mike's battlefield treatment.*

*Mike said he was humbled to be awarded the Silver Star and added, "I was more concerned about the three guys who were hit that day. I didn't go to Iraq to earn a medal or be a hero. I just wanted to do my job and to make sure my guys came home alive even if I had to sacrifice mine."*

# From Thug to Hero

## CORPORAL MARCO MARTÍNEZ

Mom,

*If you are reading this, I'm dead. Don't be mad, because I'm not mad. I'm sorry for all the grief I caused you in my middle school and high school years. I love you very much. Please bury me in the Arlington or Albuquerque military cemeteries. I'll see you in heaven.*

— *Marco*

Like many of his fellow Marines, Corporal Marco Martínez wrote a death note to a loved one as his unit prepared for the 2003 invasion of Iraq. The letter, which was turned in to the chaplain, would be sent only if Martínez were killed — a prospect he didn't want to think about. There were a lot of things he didn't want to think about, especially the teenage years he wasted before turning his life around.

Marco grew up as an army brat, living with his parents and triplet sisters on various military bases. His father, Marco Martínez Sr., was a 20-year U.S. Army Ranger. Although he looked up to his dad, Marco rebelled and fell in with the wrong crowd in Albuquerque, New Mexico. Before reaching high school, he had joined a gang and turned into a gun-toting, trash-talking, car-stealing thug who proudly sported on his back a gang tattoo that proclaimed, *Mi Vida Loca* (Spanish for "my crazy life"). He was also a tagger — a punk who spray-painted graffiti on everything from school buses to apartment buildings.

Even after the family moved to Las Cruces, New Mexico, the aimless youth still found trouble, once getting caught in the middle of a gunfight while cruising with a gang member. His pals were always up to no good. One by one, his buddies were arrested for various crimes, and another was sent to state prison for five years.

Barely making C's in high school, Marco didn't take learning seriously. No wonder some teachers coldly told him, "You're not going to amount to anything" and "Your future is a dead end."

But then one day Marco saw a Marine in person for the first time in his life. Walking down the school hallway was recruiter Staff Sergeant Javier Márquez, a six-foot-tall, barrel-chested, forearm-bulging Mexican-American. Marco felt in awe — and also felt worthless. *Compared to him, I'm nothing but a loser,* the high school junior thought.

That night, he did some serious soul-searching. *What am I going to do with my life? Work some minimum-wage job for-*

*ever? I can do better than that.* Needing time to think, he hopped into his car and drove around Las Cruces. He ended up gazing at the window of the U.S. Marine Corps recruiting office. A poster caught his eye: "If everybody could get into the Marines, it wouldn't be the Marines." The words were next to a picture of a drill instructor standing at attention, holding his sword.

A few days later, before dinner, Marco announced to his parents, "Mom, Dad, I have to tell you something."

"What did you do this time?" his mother asked warily.

"I'm going to join the Marine Corps!"

His father shook the young man's hand and said, "Marco, this is the only thing that you have done that I fully support."

Because he was only 17 and still had another year of high school left, he couldn't join immediately. But with Márquez's guidance, the teenager began conditioning himself mentally and physically. "For the Marine Corps, the minimum you have to do is your very best," the recruiter told him. For the first time ever, Marco worked hard in school and began earning straight A's. His once-shiftless life now had a focus. He had a goal to achieve. Instead of joining homecoming festivities, he took a physical fitness test. Rather than attend prom night, he ran six miles and studied Marine lore. A few weeks after graduation, he was on his way to boot camp.

The training was harder than Marco ever imagined, but he survived the grueling boot camp and earned the right to wear the coveted eagle, globe, and anchor insignia of the U.S. Marine Corps.

When he returned home on leave before heading off to the School of Infantry, his loser friends couldn't believe he was now a trained warrior. Some made fun of him, but he didn't care. He was no longer one of them — and proud of it. None had a decent job or had done anything to improve his life. He, on the other hand, planned to make his mark in the world, but he didn't know what it would be.

And now here he was, a 21-year-old corporal in Second Squad, First Platoon, Company G, Second Battalion, Fifth Marines, moments away from the invasion of Iraq. Unable to sleep, he stepped out of his tent at 1:30 A.M. and laid out his gear. Then he prayed: "Dear God, please stay with me during battle. Watch over me and give me the strength to survive." As he prayed, he took out a small bottle of holy water that his mother had given him before he deployed overseas. He sprinkled the holy water on himself, his flak jacket, helmet, weapon, and other gear. "If I'm to meet the sword of death, make it quick and precise. Help me do the right thing if I ever get confused in battle, and I ask that my rounds be well aimed and that they pierce the hearts of my enemies." In his right breast pocket, he buttoned up a rosary.

On March 20, 2003, the mighty American forces stormed into Iraq. Martínez and 17 fellow leathernecks were crammed into an amtrac. As part of a tactical formation of other vehicles, their amtrac roared across the border to their first objective and secured the oil fields in the southern city of ar-Rumaylah. Penetrating farther into Iraq, the Marines began to see just how devastating American tanks and air strikes had been. Looking out from two open doors on top of the amtrac,

Martínez saw corpses, flaming enemy tanks, and buildings turned to rubble. He coughed and gagged from air thick with the smell of burning oil, chemicals, smoke — and death.

As the Americans closed in on Baghdad, resistance became fiercer from the Republican Guard (an elite force of the Iraqi army) and Arab guerillas known as the *fedayeen.* Before Martínez's unit began patrolling the narrow, treacherous streets of the city, an officer told his squad leaders, "You are to take out anybody displaying any type of aggression toward U.S. forces. Everybody in the area is considered hostile. Contact is imminent." This was going to be the ultimate baptism under fire for Martínez. And he was ready when he and his fellow Marines engaged in several skirmishes and endured a mortar attack.

On April 12, intelligence reports indicated that fedayeen fighters were gathering north of Baghdad in the town of al-Tarmiyah, so Company G's First Platoon was ordered to do a recon. Each of the three squads piled into its own amtrac and rode 45 minutes to a bridge that led into the town. The amtracs containing First and Third squads crossed the bridge while Second Squad waited in its vehicle on the near side.

Shortly after crossing over, members of the other two squads got out of their amtracs. One squad set up security positions while the other conducted a reconnaissance of the immediate area.

Martínez and his comrades passed the time anxiously in the dark in their amtrac. After 10 tense minutes, they heard back-to-back explosions.

More than 200 fedayeen, Republican Guard, and foreign terrorists had joined forces in the town to spring a brutal ambush on the vastly outnumbered Marines. The enemy launched the surprise attack by firing two RPGs. One scored a direct hit on Third Squad's amtrac, severely wounding the gunner, driver, and mechanic. Then the militants opened fire from a line of buildings and homes on both sides of the street.

"They're getting hit up the road!" yelled Lance Corporal Tim Tardif, the squad leader. "We've got to help them!"

Martínez and members of his squad took deep breaths as their vehicle rolled across the bridge to join in the fight. He began hearing a few loud *plinks* on the right side. "They're shooting at us," he said. An outburst of bullets pummeled the armor sides of the vehicle, sounding like stones shaking in a tin can.

After their amtrac crossed the bridge, Tardif shouted, "Ready to dismount!"

When the vehicle came to a stop, it was nearly hit by an RPG that blew down a power line. The amtrac dropped its back ramp, flooding the inside with sunlight. "Go! Go! Go!" Tardif ordered.

*When I run out, I'm going to die*, Martínez thought. *There's got to be a sniper out there locked in on us, ready to pick us off when we exit.*

As soon as his boots hit the ground, Martínez felt the earth shake from the impact of enemy mortar rounds. His nose twitched from the acrid smell of gunpowder. His ears buzzed from the screams of RPGs hurtling through the kill zone, the deafening sounds of gunfire, and the shouts of enemy fighters yelling in Arabic. He saw muzzle flashes wherever he looked — from open windows of buildings, from rooftops, and from the tall elephant grass all around him. Fedayeen fighters, decked out in white ninja-style clothing, were popping out of spider holes and shooting at the Marines.

The squad had to dash across 200 yards of open terrain under intense fire. Because Martínez was the grenadier, the 5-foot 10-inch, 155-pound Marine was carrying 70 pounds of gear and ammo. Yet his strong legs carried him safely to a nearby field. The Marines formed a firing line at the swift-moving fedayeen, who scampered from point to point, each carrying only an AK-47 and one magazine.

In the initial chaos, Tardif settled on a course of action. The Marine philosophy of dealing with ambushes is to "assault through them." That involves a leapfrog maneuver in which half the squad lays down fire while the other half advances. Tardif led his squad in an attack on the buildings to their right. He and Martínez moved through the grass and crossed the road with their M16s on semiautomatic.

*If you come at the enemy with ferocity, then they'll start to cower,* Martínez told himself. *If you show fear, they will smell it. The only thing these extremists understand is violence.*

Martínez, who was the leader of the first fire team, kept shooting at the enemy. Nearby, another team set up the squad's SMAW (shoulder-fired multipurpose assault weapon) to blast a hole through an eight-foot-high adobe wall that surrounded the nearest home.

Martínez turned around and saw a terrorist, who had been hiding in the tall grass, lob a grenade. It hit Tardif's knee and bounced off.

"Grenade!" yelled Tardif as he dived for cover. The grenade rolled a few yards away and then exploded, sending shrapnel deep into his right leg.

"Nooo!" screamed Martínez. In a rage, he shot and killed the grenade thrower and also another terrorist as they fled through the grass. Then he raced over to Tardif, who was bleeding badly. Tardif tried to stand up but collapsed. "It feels like a hot iron is burning in my leg," said the squad leader. Martínez saw Tardif's thigh bone through the wide-open wound. With no corpsman nearby, Lance Corporal Elmer Miguel, who had some medical training, immediately began applying a pressure bandage on it. The rest of the squad laid down withering fire and killed attackers who were jumping out from their hiding places. Then Tardif and the team continued their assault on enemy positions. Meanwhile, hundreds of yards away, members of the First and Third squads were clearing houses.

During a brief lull, Tardif collapsed from his wounds. One of the Marines asked, "What are we going to do next?"

Everyone looked at Martínez, who was next in line to assume leadership of the squad. *We're getting shot at from every angle*, he thought. *The rest of the platoon is too far away and engaged in their own fights, so we can't get any help from them. That's okay. I'm prepared for this. I know Tim's job and the others' as well. I'm ready for this.*

Ordering his comrades to get in a wide circle around Tardif, Martínez knelt down, held Tardif's hand, and looked at his pale face. Tardif kept fading in and out and could barely speak. *My God, he's going to bleed out and die*, Martínez thought.

"Hang in there," he said to Tardif. "We're going to get you out of here."

Seeing the Marines tending to their wounded leader, the terrorists began firing at them from the second-story window of a nearby house. As Tardif, who had passed out, was carried to a safer location, Martínez told his men, "We have houses to clear and a payback to deliver."

Outside the first house, Martínez told members of the second fire team, "Once my fire team goes in, if you see anyone else try to go in or out, shoot them." Martínez and three Marines burst into the front door of the house where more than a dozen militants were hiding. Every room the leathernecks entered had at least one terrorist shooting at them. Martínez was firing at such close range — once while the enemy was on the other side of a table — that he could smell their breath, see the pores of their skin, and make out the color of their eyes. Bullets flew by his head but never touched him. He was quick on the draw. *Kill them before they kill me,* he kept telling himself. He never felt scared because he kept telling himself, *I'm with my Marines.*

Sweat soaked his sleeves. His ears were ringing from the amplified sound of the gunshots. All he could hear were the sounds inside himself — hard gulping and heavy breathing — and the muffled yells of the terrorists. As he led the way up the stairs, he felt his heart beat faster with each step, because he had no way of knowing who, and how many, lay in wait at the top. On the second floor, he and his fire team eliminated the remaining militants.

The four Marines had wiped out 15 terrorists in the house. *I've never been prouder of my fire team,* he thought as they took a breather on the flat roof. *They stayed cool and methodical through it all.*

Suddenly, his team started taking heavy rounds from fighters in a house across the street that was surrounded by an adobe wall, so Martínez ordered the SMAW gunners to blast a hole in it. When they did, he and his men scrambled out of the house they had just cleared. They returned fire while sprinting through the hole in the wall and into the front yard of the next house. The militants popped out of their spider holes in the yard like a swarm of insects, but the Marines mowed them down.

Behind the home was a guesthouse where five fully armed terrorists were shooting at the Marines. A few thin palm trees provided the only cover in the yard, so Martínez hid behind one. He stood erect and held his breath, trying to make himself as skinny as possible. While the rest of the squad slipped into the house, a flurry of bullets whizzed past both sides of the tree trunk that he was using for cover.

He glanced directly behind him at the wall that the Marines had just breached. The only portion of the wall not riddled with enemy bullets was a tall, narrow, two-foot-wide patch that mirrored the outline of his tree trunk.

Martínez was now less than 50 feet from the guesthouse, firing somewhat blindly at the militants inside. He couldn't step out from behind the palm tree to get off good shots because he would be exposed and likely killed.

Then he heard the enemy's AK-47 jam. *Here's my chance!* He jumped from behind the tree and charged the guesthouse while Corporals Paul Gardner and Mickey Jaramillo and Lance Corporal Marcelino Garcia laid down suppressive fire. Halfway to the guesthouse, Martínez heard the AK-47 reengage and resume firing.

He was stranded. *I'm going to die for sure.* He sprinted toward the nearest palm tree about 25 yards away, knowing that he was making a perfect target. As he ran, he spotted an enemy's loaded RPG launcher lying on the ground. It had been dropped by a militant who had been shot and wounded but had run off. Martínez slowed down and scooped up the weapon, then reached the safety of the palm tree. He was surprised he hadn't taken a bullet yet.

Now he was in possession of an enemy weapon that he had never touched before and hadn't the slightest idea how to use. *If I could figure out how to fire this thing, I could destroy the building. This could be the deciding factor on whether we get home or not. How cool would that be to shoot the bad guys with their own weapon.*

He examined the RPG and fumbled with it until the rocket snapped firmly in place in the launcher. Placing the weapon on his shoulder, he stepped out from behind the tree, kneeled down, and squeezed the trigger. But nothing happened. Ducking behind the tree, he reloaded the rocket, checked the sights, and put it back on his shoulder again before once again exposing himself to enemy fire. He pulled the trigger, but like before, it failed to fire. *Damn! Is it a dud?* He was about to toss it aside when he finally figured out the problem. *The launcher has a dual-trigger system.*

But then he heard Gardner scream and crash to the ground about seven yards away. *He's been shot!* A bullet had ripped into the left side of Gardner's torso, clipping his spine. He couldn't move and was choking on his own blood. The militants tried to finish him off, firing rounds that were striking only inches away from him.

*If I'm going to shoot this thing, I better do it now*, Martínez thought, *because if I don't, they're going to kill Gardner.*

Martínez pointed the RPG at the terrorists in the guesthouse, braced for the kickback, and squeezed the trigger. To his great satisfaction, the rocket zoomed across the yard, tearing into the structure, killing two of the five shooters inside.

Most importantly, the direct hit bought the Marines a 10-second break in the action so they could reach Gardner, who was paralyzed from the waist down. As the leathernecks began dragging him out of the line of fire, the three surviving terrorists started shooting at them.

"Oh, no, you don't!" growled Martínez. He charged out from behind the tree and ran directly toward the guesthouse while firing his M16. Garcia and Jaramillo provided him with covering fire. But when he was 15 yards from the terrorists, he ran out of ammo. He let go of his weapon, which still hung from a sling around his body, and sprinted toward the guesthouse. He was expecting a bullet to strike him, expecting that fatal second when his life would be snuffed out. *If I die, I die*, he thought. *There'll be another Marine to take over.*

While on the run, he prepped a hand grenade. He could hear the shooters yelling in Arabic as they ducked down and fired their rounds out the window without looking.

He reached the outer wall of the structure, and then flung the grenade as hard as he could into the nearest open window. He stood with his back pressed against the wall, waiting for the blast. The concussion from the explosion jolted him unlike anything he had ever experienced. The blast hammered his eardrums, causing liquid to run out of his ears. His head pounded and he felt wobbly, nauseous, and disoriented. For about five seconds, he wondered if he was dead.

But he regained his senses and his balance. Then he reloaded his M16 and walked behind the blown-up guesthouse. As he turned the corner, he spotted a wounded fedayeen fighter start to aim an AK-47 at him. Martínez got off four quick shots and killed the terrorist.

The three-hour firefight was winding down. A helicopter arrived to carry out Tardif and Gardner, who were still alive but fading fast. (Tardif recovered and eventually returned to his unit. Gardner remained paralyzed from his waist down.) As the wounded were being loaded up, three militants jumped out of the nearby bushes and began shooting. The Marines killed them.

Returning to their base, Martínez called a squad meeting and told his comrades, "I'm writing up each one of you for at least a NAM [Navy and Marine Corps Achievement Medal] with a V for valor.

"As long as I'm with you guys, I will never fear for my life. The tactical precision displayed out there today makes me know we could make it out of anything the enemy has to throw at us. I want you guys to know that it's an honor and a privilege to be your squad leader."

The U.S. Marine Corps recognized the extraordinary heroism under fire displayed in Iraq on April 12, 2003, by Corporal Marco Martínez. On May 3, 2004, Secretary of the Navy Gordon England pinned the Navy Cross on Martínez's chest, making him the first Hispanic-American since the Vietnam War to be awarded the medal.

According to the official citation, "By his outstanding display of decisive leadership, unlimited courage in the face of heavy enemy fire, and utmost devotion to duty, Corporal Martínez reflected great credit upon himself and upheld the highest traditions of the Marine Corps."

After he left the military, Martínez wrote the book Hard Corps (published by Crown Forum) that detailed how he transformed himself from a lawless gang member to a courageous Marine hero.

For displaying leadership and courage while seriously injured during the fierce assault, Lance Corporal Tim Tardif was awarded the Silver Star in 2004.

# In the
# Line of Fire

## HOSPITAL CORPSMAN SECOND CLASS
## JUAN RUBIO

**H**ospital Corpsman Juan "Doc" Rubio gripped his M16 rifle as the boat he was riding in glided down the muddy Euphrates River. He kept his eyes peeled along the reed-choked banks, looking for any sign of another ambush.

The Marines he was with already had been struck earlier in the day when they shot their way out of a riverfront attack. One of the Marines had been hit in the leg and brought back to the battle-aid station near Haditha Dam, where Rubio had patched him up. Now they were back on the water, this time with more troops.

Rubio was not just a hospital corpsman. He was a fighter, too, attached to the Fourth Platoon, Small Craft Company, First Marines, which operated 40-foot-long camouflaged boats powered by twin souped-up 440-horsepower racing engines.

The boats, which carried a squad of 20 and a mix of heavy and light machine guns, could zoom up to 50 miles an hour, turn on a dime, and stop in a boat length.

The crafts patrolled the always dangerous Euphrates morning, noon, and night. The Marines' mission: to intercept insurgents ferrying arms down the river, to thwart mortar and RPG attacks from sandbars and islands, and to uncover caches of weapons hidden in the riverbanks.

Since their arrival in Iraq in the fall of 2004, Rubio and his comrades had been attacked — sometimes from both sides of the river — at least five times a week on their thrice daily patrols. Rubio expected more of the same today. The enemy didn't care that it was New Year's Day 2005.

First came a few potshots from the tall reeds on the riverbank, then more bullets and several RPGs. Rubio and the leathernecks countered by laying down fire wherever they saw muzzle flashes. On the transom of each boat, a .50-caliber machine gun, which is capable of sawing a car in two with its sausage-size rounds, riddled the shoreline. So, too, did the dependable M240B medium machine gun, a weapon accurate for up to one mile. The insurgents quickly fled after the boats' heavy machine guns each churned out an incredible 50 rounds per second through six rotating barrels.

When the gunfire ebbed, the Marines leaped off their boats to hunt down their attackers. Rubio saw blood splatters and drag marks on the ground, so he knew some of the insurgents had been injured in the firefight. He and his comrades started tracking the bloody trail. About 50 yards from the river, they encountered more enemy fire, but easily pushed their way forward.

This was the same area where four days earlier the team had searched the riverbank and nearby buildings for bombs and weapons. Every loose bit of soil was turned over, every ramshackle hut was probed. The Marines' painstaking work paid off big-time: They uncovered two large caches of weapons, high-explosive rounds, mortars, dynamite, and devices for IEDs.

"We obviously ticked them off after taking all those weapons the other day," Rubio told radioman Lance Corporal Brian Parrello. Rubio made a point of staying close to him so that if there were any casualties within the squadron, he would be the first to hear over the radio, "We need Doc."

Rubio had been helping people in need ever since he was an emergency-room technician in his hometown of San Angelo, Texas. Hoping to advance his career, he enlisted in the U.S. Navy as a corpsman. Rubio was stationed at Bethesda Naval Hospital in Maryland when terrorists on 9/11 crashed a jetliner into the Pentagon. He was dispatched to the chaotic scene where, as a member of an emergency medical-response team, he treated the injured. Days later, in New York City, he served aboard the hospital ship USNS *Comfort*, which was opened to recovery workers who were sifting through the remains of the World Trade Center. In 2003, when President George W. Bush made the decision to invade Iraq, Rubio, then 28, volunteered to be a corpsman for the U.S. Marine Corps (which has no corpsmen of its own). During the invasion, Rubio encountered deadly firefights. He developed a reputation as a navy man with the heart and soul of a Marine, a cool professional who saved lives with his battlefield first-aid training and killed insurgents with his sharpshooting skills.

When his tour was over, Rubio volunteered again to return to Iraq, this time with the Small Craft Company. He believed his combat experience and medical training would help the untested young unit, which was manned mostly by Marines under the age of 21. Parrello, for example, was only 19.

Now here it was, New Year's Day, and they were on the hunt for insurgents. Rubio, Parrello, and the other Marines pushed another 100 yards farther inland. They reached an area that had five buildings, including a pump house that sent water from the river to the irrigation ditches of nearby farms. Three pipes, each about a foot in diameter with one stacked on top of the other two, stretched from the pump house beyond the other buildings.

The Marines split into two groups, half angling off to the left and the other half to the right. Rubio, Parrello, Captain Jonathan Kuniholm, and Gunnery Sergeant Brian Vinciguerra were near one another when they came upon a five-foot-high wall. They all stopped, suspecting enemy fighters were lying in wait on the other side.

Kuniholm, an engineer and Marine reservist attached to the unit, spotted a five-gallon aluminum oilcan on top of the wall. Pointing to the can, he told Rubio, "The insurgents have been using markers like this. They place them by an IED so when a convoy or foot patrol gets near the marker, the insurgents set off the bomb by a remote. I remember a similar can had been used to mark a bomb a week ago. Let's move back."

Rubio turned around and noticed that Parrello hadn't heard the warning because he was busy on his radio giving the coordinates of their position to the remaining crew on the boats. The ground combat unit wasn't supposed to move beyond 150 yards from their craft, but this time they did in their pursuit of the terrorists.

"Parrello, we need to get away from the wall," Rubio said. He grabbed the radioman by the collar and spun him around.

They had taken only a few steps when a huge explosion lifted them off their feet. The blast knocked Parrello into Rubio and hurled them against the side of a building, knocking them both out.

When Rubio started to regain consciousness, he couldn't see anything at first other than what seemed like a dot on a blank screen. Slowly his vision improved, and the range of what he could see grew wider. But his hearing was altered because of loud ringing in his ears. His body felt like it was burning, but a quick scan of his arms and legs showed he hadn't been burned. He figured he wasn't too hurt, although he was bleeding and still felt burning sensations in his arms and legs. *Must be nothing more than the soreness caused by the blast*, he thought. He started crawling away.

As the ringing subsided, he began hearing the roar of RPGs, AK-47s, RPKs, M16s, and M203s. *Geez, we were lured into this ambush*, he thought, seeing dirt kick up around him. *And a very well-planned one.* He was awed by the massive volume of fire that had pinned down the Marines.

By now, he had fully regained his vision. *I need to make sure my Marines are safe!* He looked around and saw that Parrello was sprawled on the ground a few yards away, bleeding badly and not moving. *Not Parrello! I've got to get to him.*

Grabbing his M16, Rubio low-crawled out to his fallen comrade, stopping every few seconds to unload a hefty number of rounds at the enemy, especially at two insurgents who were firing RPGs. One of the projectiles crashed into the building behind Rubio, flinging debris and shrapnel, some of which peppered the corpsman.

Ignoring the pain and the bullets that were aimed at him, Rubio fired off several more rounds and watched three insurgents fall. In the clamor of combat, he could hear the steady pops of M16s and knew the leathernecks were providing him with covering fire. *Just think about what I need to do to save Parrello,* he told himself. *Don't worry about getting shot.*

Rubio shouted, "Parrello! Parrello! It's me . . . Doc. Can you hear me?" *No response.*

Rubio opened up Parrello's flak jacket and cut away his cammies to expose the injuries. He removed the radio, which had been damaged by the explosion, and threw it toward the pipes, where it was retrieved by a Marine. Even though the radio didn't work, he didn't want the insurgents to get it.

A quick examination of Parrello revealed several broken ribs, internal injuries, and a shredded right arm. *God, he must have absorbed 90 percent of the blast,* the corpsman thought. *He's in bad shape.* "C'mon, Parrello, talk to me, man."

Parrello coughed, winced, and opened his eyes. "Doc," he said weakly, "are you all right?"

"Brother, don't worry about me. Don't worry about me."

"Oh, I hurt all over," Parrello muttered. "It's hard to breathe."

"You're going to be okay. I'm going to fix you up." Rubio injected him with morphine to deaden the pain and then bandaged his injuries.

"Give him cover!" a Marine shouted. They let loose with a blizzard of bullets as Rubio grabbed hold of the radioman's shoulders and then carefully dragged him for about 20 yards. When he reached the pipes, Rubio spotted an insurgent peeking out from behind a building, aiming his AK-47 right at them. The corpsman whipped his M16 into position, fired, and killed him.

Rubio pulled Parrello over the pipes and hauled him to a safe spot behind a building where Fourth Platoon Commander Lieutenant Andrew Thomas and Sergeant Vasci were firing their weapons.

Just as he was beginning to work on Parrello some more, Rubio heard, "The captain's been hit! The captain is down!"

Turning to the two Marines next to him, Rubio said, "I've got to go back and get him." He gave them instructions on what to do to keep Parrello stabilized, adding, "Stay with him and talk to him. Hold pressure here on his arm and keep it elevated. I'll be right back." Rubio had faith in his Marines because he had trained 18 of them in combat lifesaving skills.

He tried to jump over the pipes, but the enemy fire was too heavy. Turning to his left, he shouted to Corporal Aguilar, "Give me cover fire!" Then off to his right, he yelled to Lance Corporal Reiman, "Cover me! I'm going to punch forward!"

As bullets flew, Rubio leaped over the pipes, squeezed off several four-round bursts, and zigzagged his way out to the captain, who was on the ground, bleeding badly. His right arm had almost been blown off below the elbow, and he was nearly in shock. Securing the mangled arm, Rubio led him back, through enemy fire, to the other side of the pump house and began treating him with Corporal Schaffer assisting.

"My arm!" Kuniholm moaned. "Is it still there?"

"Yes, sir, and I'm working on it," Rubio replied.

"Doc, will I still be able to play the guitar?"

"Yes, you will, sir. You're going to go home and play the guitar and hold your kids." Rubio always tried to reinforce victims' morale and lift their spirits, because when the adrenaline is pumping, they don't fully grasp how serious their injuries are. He offered comforting words to divert their attention from their wounds.

After reassuring the captain, Rubio tied a tourniquet about an inch above Kuniholm's elbow and applied an absorbing powder to stop the bleeding. He put a cravat (a triangular bandage) to hold the captain's arm in place. Then he did a sweep of Kuniholm's body to make sure he had no bullet wounds. When the captain was stabilized, Rubio cut his sleeve and was preparing to start an IV. That's when Schaffer said, "He's bleeding! He's bleeding from another wound above his elbow!"

"What color is it?"

"It's bright red."

"That means it's blood from a severed artery. Whatever you do, hold pressure."

Rubio grabbed a tourniquet and tossed it to Schaffer. "Go into your first-aid pack, get a cravat, and tie it tight as you can where the bleeding is, just above the tourniquet. As soon as I get this IV secured, I'll deal with it."

Kuniholm's eyes grew big, and he said, "Slow down, Doc. Slow down. You're going too fast."

"This is the only way I work, sir. If I go any slower, my ADHD [attention deficit hyperactivity disorder] is going to kick in, and I'm going to lose track of what I'm doing."

The captain stared at the corpsman and, despite the magnitude of his injuries, began to laugh.

Once Rubio secured the IV, he scrambled over to Kuniholm's right side to take care of the other wound.

"Doc! Doc! Gunny's been hit!" a Marine yelled. "We need you over here!"

Gunnery Sergeant Brian Vinciguerra was staggering out in the open after being wounded in the right hand and arm by an RPG and machine-gunfire.

As he reached for his M16, Rubio told Schaffer, "Keep the captain alert and talk to him. I've got to get Gunny."

Directing cover fire at muzzle flashes in a tree line, Rubio crossed over two unsecured areas, popping off rounds as he ran. He reached Vinciguerra, who was rapidly losing blood from his wounds, and brought him safely to the other side of a building. Rubio then stabilized him and tied a cravat around the wounds. He called over Lance Corporal Powell, one of his combat lifesavers, and told him, "Make sure you keep Gunny alert. I'm going back to help Parrello."

Rubio rushed over to his comrade and saw he had taken a turn for the worse, going in and out of consciousness. *We need to evacuate him and the others right now!*

The boats were nearby, but with the platoon's radio out of commission, the crews onboard weren't sure where to shoot. Instead, two runners delivered messages back and forth and helped direct fire from the boats' guns.

While calling for cover fire, Rubio and several Marines began moving the casualties from the ambush site to the shoreline. They had trained for this over and over. They were still under fire when Aguilar and Rubio carried Parrello to one of the boats.

As Gunny and the captain were being placed on another boat, Rubio told the crew, "Give me minute-by-minute updates of those two while I work on Parrello."

When everyone was aboard, Lieutenant Thomas gave the order, "Punch out! Punch out!" The boats' engines roared to life, and the crafts sped upstream toward three Humvees waiting to whisk the casualties to the battle-aid station (BAS) where doctors could administer more care.

During the ride back, Parrello lost consciousness and stopped breathing. Rubio quickly realized that one of Parrello's broken ribs had pierced the area between the lung and the chest wall, causing the lung to collapse because it could not fill up with air. "Oh, no, you don't," Rubio said. "I'm not about to lose you."

As the speeding boat skimmed the water, the calm corpsman performed a delicate emergency procedure that involved inserting a needle between Parrello's third and fourth ribs to let out the air surrounding his collapsed lung. After Rubio purposely punctured the chest cavity, he heard a gush of air. Once the air escaped the chest cavity, the lung was able to expand.

The radioman began to breathe again and fluttered his eyes.

"Yes, yes! You're back!" But Rubio knew Parrello had serious internal bleeding that the corpsman couldn't treat because it required an emergency room. *I can't keep him alive much longer.*

When they arrived on shore, he put Parrello into a Humvee. "Hurry!" he shouted to the driver. "We're running out of time!" They had to drive past the massive dam and go through unsecured territory to get to the BAS.

"Are . . . the . . . other . . . Marines . . . okay?" Parrello asked with labored breath.

"Yes, they'll be fine."

"Will . . . I . . . be . . . okay?"

"Sure you will, man." *Why aren't we there yet? He's starting to fade.* "Don't give up, Parrello," he urged. "You can do it."

"I'm . . . hurting. . . . It's . . . so . . . hard . . . to . . . breathe."

"I know, Brother. We're almost there. Think of home, think of your family."

Like other members of the unit, Rubio was fond of the easygoing 19-year-old, who enlisted in the Marines directly from high school in West Milford, New Jersey, where he starred on the hockey team.

Rubio cradled Parrello's head. *He's dying, and there's nothing else I can do other than give him more morphine. Damn it! Please don't die on me.* "Everybody is pulling for you, Brother."

At the BAS, the casualties were put aboard medevac helicopters for the trip to the closest military hospital. Rubio squeezed Parrello's hand and said, "I'll see you soon. Stay strong." *Don't die, Parrello. Don't . . .*

"Hey, Doc, we need you," said Corporal Stoops, running up to Rubio. "We're going back out there to finish the job."

Rubio took a deep breath and thought, *I'll have time to worry about Parrello later. Right now I've got to go back to work.* He reloaded his med bag, gathered other supplies, and limped out to the Humvee where Stoops and Corporal Stoddard were waiting. In all the turmoil of battle and his feverish efforts to save the wounded, Rubio forgot how much he hurt. But he refused to dwell on the pain.

On the ride to the boats, Stoddard looked at the corpsman, who was sitting in the backseat, and said, "Doc, you've been hit in the leg. You've got blood on you."

Rubio was accustomed to having other soldiers' blood on his uniform. "No, no, it's not my blood," he said. "It's someone else's."

"No, Doc. Your pants are ripped," said Stoddard, pulling back a hole in the corpsman's cammies. "I can see bone in your wound."

Rubio looked down and said, "Oh, geez. You're right."

Stoddard yelled to Stoops, who was driving the Humvee, "We gotta turn back! Doc's hurt!"

Stoops slammed on the brakes so hard that Rubio flew from the backseat to the front. "What are you trying to do, Stoops, kill me?" the corpsman complained.

"I'm sorry, Doc," Stoops apologized.

"Just get me back in one piece."

Rubio was taken by helicopter to a hospital in al-Assad, where he was treated for a concussion and shrapnel injuries from his left shoulder to his elbow and in both legs. He also had wounds in the back of his head from flying fragments caused by the RPG blast. The doctors removed what they could, including a small metal splinter that had been embedded in his head since a firefight a month earlier.

The corpsman was still in the hospital when he got an update that he didn't want to hear: Parrello had died while being medevaced. The news rocked Rubio, and he broke down and wept. *I've lost my brother. I've lost a good kid. If it hadn't been for him, if he hadn't taken the brunt of the explosion, I wouldn't be alive. I owe my life to him.*

Despite his grief, Rubio was determined to return to his unit. But the doctors had other plans. "Some of the shrapnel is embedded too deeply in your leg," a physician told him. "It will require major surgery to remove all of it, and you'll have to recover back in the States."

"I don't want to leave my Marines," said Rubio, who had three months left on his current tour. "I heard that many people can live with shrapnel inside them for years and years. Can I live with it in my leg?"

"Yes, but you're going to feel pain from time to time. And it's going to continue bothering you."

"That's okay. Bandage me up and send me back to my guys." Three days later, Rubio caught a convoy and linked up with his platoon. He finished out his tour the way he started it — by trying to save the lives of his Marines.

* * *

Jonathan Kuniholm, who was promoted to major in the U.S. Marine Corps Reserve, had his arm amputated. He now uses an advanced prosthesis that allows him to do many things, including fly his own plane and strum a guitar. Trained in biomedical engineering, he is helping to develop new technology for amputees.

Gunnery Sergeant Brian Vinciguerra recovered from his injuries and credits Rubio with saving his life: "He's my hero, and without him I wouldn't be standing here today."

For his actions on that fateful day, Hospital Corpsman Second Class Juan Rubio was awarded the Silver Star.

Rubio, who often feels the pain from the shrapnel embedded in his leg, said he is humbled by the honor. "I was only doing what any corpsman would do in that situation. I proudly wear it for the other corpsmen."

However, he added, the real heroes of this war are the children of servicemen and servicewomen — children such as his sons, Joshua and Matthew, who were ten and eight respectively when they attended the medal ceremony. "Those in the military are trained to preserve and protect, but our children aren't trained to do without their father, mother, older brother, or sister," Rubio said. "They have to lie in their beds, not knowing if their loved one will ever come home. They pray and pray every night. That takes honor and courage."

# When Death Came Calling

## LANCE CORPORAL MARK CAMP

Lance Corporal Mark Camp stood in the top hatch of a rolling amtrac, his hand resting on his weapon, his eyes darting left and right. He and his fellow gunner were scanning the drab, dusty countryside for any signs of trouble as the convoy headed toward its next mission.

It was the morning of May 11, 2005 — day five of Operation Matador, a weeklong, door-to-door hunt to root out insurgents and foreign fighters in the dangerous al-Anbar province in western Iraq.

In some ways, it was hard for Camp to believe he was here in Iraq. Hadn't it been just four months ago that he was sitting in history class at Ohio State University? Sure, he knew his chances of going to war were good because he was a member of Lima Company, a Marine Reserve unit out of

Columbus, Ohio, part of the Third Battalion, Twenty-fifth Marines. One weekend a month he trained with police officers, construction workers, tradesmen, college students, and other young reservists just getting their start in life. Then in January 2005, they were plucked from their daily routines when Lima Company was called up. By March, the unit was shipped to Iraq, where it was attached to the Fourth Marine Division.

Camp and his fellow leathernecks patrolled insurgent strongholds along the Euphrates River valley and the Syrian border, a lawless region the size of West Virginia and known by coalition forces as the Wild West. Part of their job was to find and block "ratlines" — routes used by terrorists to smuggle weapons from Syria into al-Anbar province.

The skirmishes his unit faced during the first two months were dealt with quickly and professionally with few injuries. The press began referring to the company as Lucky Lima, and the name stuck in the media. Eventually, fighting turned tougher and grimmer. The Marines had encountered suicidal militants who had dug in and fought with deadly road-side bombs, sniper attacks, and several well-planned ambushes.

On this day, Camp, his head and shoulders sticking above the hatch of the squad's amtrac, remained on high alert. The rest of the 17 men in the vehicle were squished thigh to thigh on hard benches in the dark below. They wouldn't see their field of combat until the rear ramp dropped down and they charged out with weapons ready. So they passed the time on the bumpy ride by munching from their ration packs, ribbing one another, or catching catnaps.

As the convoy passed hamlets and villages, Camp was relieved to see people going about their business. *That's a good sign,* he thought. Generally, the population knows to stay away if there is going to be an ambush. Camp tried to relax, thinking, *The civilians seem friendly enough. It's supposed to be a safe road, so nothing bad should happen.* When he saw kids playing and waving, he waved back. *I wish I had candy to throw them.*

But as the convoy neared the next town, he noticed there wasn't a soul outside other than a stray dog or two. *Uh-oh. I have a bad feeling about this.* He wondered if the jitters he was suddenly experiencing were because he was still dealing with the tragedy that took place three days earlier. *Or maybe,* he thought, *it's the nightmare.* The night before this mission, his girlfriend, Maria, appeared in a troubling dream, warning him that something terrible was going to happen, but that he would survive it.

"Hey, guys," Camp shouted down to his squad. "It's too quiet out there, and I don't see anyone. This doesn't look good."

As a safety measure, he slipped his goggles, which had been resting on his helmet, down over his eyes. But he didn't bother putting on his fireproof gloves, which remained in his backpack.

The platoon, in its row of amtracs, rumbled toward the Euphrates River near the Syrian border when . . . *Ka-BOOM!* An IED — believed to be two buried bombs stacked one on top of the other — exploded, launching Camp's amtrac several feet off the ground. The force catapulted the other gunner who was with him through the air and into a nearby field.

The blast enveloped the vehicle in flames, sending orange balls of fire soaring above the trees. A flash lit Camp's hands and face on fire. For a brief moment, he felt weightless before everything came crashing down. He tumbled into the cabin of the amtrac and landed on Lance Corporal Carl Schneider's legs. Inside, shrapnel and flames tore through the Marines, who were shouting in anguish.

*I'm on fire! I'm on fire!* Frantically, Camp waved his hands and banged them on his chest and legs, trying to snuff out the flames. Then he beat on his burning cheeks with his arms. Smelling and tasting the fuel that had splattered on his face, he thought, *The fuel tank must have blown up and splashed fuel on us.*

His face stinging and hands burning, the dazed Camp looked around for a way to escape. It was hard to breathe or see because of the choking smoke. Marines had been thrown helter-skelter, and their bodies were tangled with the limbs of unconscious comrades. "Get out! Get out before our rounds start cooking off [exploding]!" Camp yelled.

"We can't get the back door open!" a leatherneck hollered back.

The stricken amtrac was turning into a flaming hot box. "Use the fire extinguisher!" Camp shouted.

"It's not working!" a Marine bellowed.

Camp cringed when he saw two leathernecks engulfed in flames and shrieking in agony. *Oh, God, I'm going to die a horrible death.* Just as bullets torched by the fire began exploding, the back door flung open and the luckiest of the Marines scrambled, dived, or rolled out. All were hurt.

Meanwhile, Marines in the other amtracs streamed from their open ramps and sprinted toward the destroyed vehicle, the metal already turning black from the fire. "Hurry! Hurry! C'mon! C'mon!" they shouted while carrying out the wounded on their backs and on stretchers. During the rescue attempts, bullets snapped from the burning hulk and traveled hundreds of feet. Sergeant Phillip Jolly rushed up and helped Camp, whose hands were still smoldering, out of the amtrac and onto a grassy area where Camp slumped to the ground.

In the field, corpsmen and other Marines feverishly worked on victims whose limbs were burned or whose torsos were bleeding from terrible shrapnel wounds.

"We passed right over it [the IED] and nothing happened," said a Marine who had been in one of the amtracs ahead of Camp's and was now helping the wounded. "Why didn't it explode earlier?"

Lance Corporal Wesley Davids, who had been blown out of the vehicle by the blast, was lying near Camp. He was gritting his teeth and in obvious pain.

"Are you all right?" Camp asked.

Davids gave him a scathing look and then pointed to his right leg — or what was left of it. The explosion had ripped off almost his entire leg.

*That* was *a pretty stupid thing to say,* Camp thought. He knew it would be useless to use a tourniquet. "I want to help you, but I don't know what to do," said Camp, holding up his burned hands. Seeing how blackened they were made him sick to his stomach. *Don't look at them anymore.*

Off to his left, Camp spotted a Marine who was on fire from his chest to his head and was rolling around on the ground. *I've got to help him!* Camp struggled to his feet and kicked dirt on him, trying to smother the flames. Just then, Camp heard a cry for help coming from inside the amtrac.

"Mark! Mark! Help me! I'm trapped! Please help me!"

Camp recognized the voice. It belonged to Private First Class Christopher Dixon, of Obetz, Ohio, a member of Camp's fire team. Dixon, 18, the youngest leatherneck in the squad, was a likable, innocent kid who loved to talk about trucks, motorcycles, and hunting.

*I need to get to him before he dies.* Camp started to limp toward the amtrac when he banged his right leg and felt a stabbing pain. He noticed for the first time that he had taken shrapnel in his right thigh. The largest piece was the top ring from an MK19 grenade round that was lodged deep in the muscle.

He stayed low as he neared the amtrac because the heat from the fire was still cooking off ammunition. Bullets flew in all directions. Burning flares and grenades rocketed into the sky and across a pasture. Although he was scared and almost certain that he would die or suffer further injury, Camp kept going. He thought about only one thing: *I've got to save Chris.*

The amtrac's front end was tilted down in the crater caused by the explosion and its back end was angled upward. When he reached the vehicle, the rear opening was now by Camp's neck. He pulled himself up inside and saw that Dixon, who had been sitting on the floor in the middle of the amtrac when it was struck by the IED, was lying in a jumble of bodies and equipment. Camp didn't see anyone else moving inside.

"Mark! Help me!" Dixon pleaded. "I've been hit by shrapnel and I'm trapped and can't move. Help me, man. I don't want to die."

"I know you're scared, Chris. I'm going to get you out. But my hands are weak because they've been burned, so you need to help me."

"I will. I will," said Dixon. "We're going to survive this, aren't we?"

"Yeah, yeah, we are." Camp pulled him up by the armpits into a sitting position and spun him around so that his head was near the door. "We're almost out of here," said Camp. He tugged on Dixon, but Dixon's leg was still snagged on something. "Come on, we're so close."

Suddenly, the vehicle was rocked by another powerful explosion that blew Camp backward out of the doorway and into the crater. Flames shot out, singeing his hands again, forcing him to beat his already burned hands against his chest to snuff out the flames.

"Chris!" Camp yelled as he scrambled to his feet. "Chris!" There was no response.

Totally focused on saving his comrade rather than dealing with his own painful injuries, Camp climbed back into the raging inferno. Exploding ammo was ricocheting inside, and flames were licking Dixon's body, which was folded over and facing away from the doorway. Camp reached out to grab the strap attached to the barrel of the gun that Dixon had slung over his back, but it was on fire.

"Chris, wake up! I can't do this without your help!" Camp jerked on Dixon's arms, his helmet, his collar, but Dixon wouldn't budge. Camp yanked harder, only to cry out in agony because of the charred skin on his hands. Whatever strength and tolerance to pain he had from the adrenaline rush following the blast was fading fast. *I'm not strong enough to get him out.* "I need some help here!" he shouted. "I need some fresh hands!"

His plea was heard by Gunnery Sergeant Chuck Hurley and Sergeant Guy Zierk, who rushed over and pulled out Camp. As they moved him away, he told them, "Forget about me. Dixon's still in there and others are, too! Get them out!"

By now the pain in Camp's hands, face, and thigh had intensified. He could no longer walk or even stand, but he was thankful to be alive. Seeing other leathernecks who were burned or injured worse than him, he was grateful that his goggles — parts of which had melted — had saved his eyesight. He glanced at the smoking, blazing amtrac and winced. It was so hot that the blackened vehicle was melting.

Then came the devastating news: Dixon was dead . . . and others were, too.

"Nooo!" moaned Camp. "Not again!" Still fresh in his mind, still hurting in his gut was the horrifying ordeal that had unfolded less than three days earlier.

On Mother's Day, May 8, the second day of Operation Matador, Camp and his company were sent to the town of Ubaydi on a house-clearing mission in an area overrun with militants. The army had been taking sniper fire while setting up a temporary bridge, so Lima Company was tasked with clearing part of the town of insurgents who were hiding or just blending in. As soon as they entered Ubaydi, the Marines were assaulted with automatic weapons and RPGs. At a former Iraqi military base, insurgents shot through windows, rooftops, and doorways and threw grenades. The loudspeakers on the mosques tried to rally the locals to fight the Americans.

Lima Company pushed through. By late in the afternoon, the unit received orders to clear out a final block of row houses. In each home that Camp entered, he wondered what he would face: a frightened defenseless family or armed terrorists lying in wait. At first, the Marines didn't find much resistance. What they did find were weapons caches, RPGs, and explosives left behind by fleeing insurgents.

Then the leathernecks came to the last house at the end of the block. Like they had at the other homes, they yelled for everyone inside to come out. At this house, no one did, which meant the Marines would have to bust down the door and charge inside.

Camp was outside the gate of the front courtyard in a prone position in case any militants tried to rush in behind the Marines. Carrying ammo pouches around his hips, he was gripping the SAW, the squad automatic weapon.

As Marines were about to kick the door open, they were met with a spray of bullets. Corporal Dustin Derga, a 24-year-old fire-team leader, was shot through his side and dropped. Lance Corporal Collen West took rounds in the lung and leg. A bullet struck the forearm of Corpsman Murray "Doc" Griffen, but he stumbled to safety. A sergeant was grazed three times by enemy rounds, including one that slammed into the side of his helmet and knocked him out.

The rounds almost hit Camp. He scrunched up by the corner of a wall and returned fire along with other members of his squad. Hurley, the platoon commander, immediately worked up a plan to retrieve the wounded. Staff Sergeant Anthony Goodwin, the 33-year-old platoon leader, turned to Camp and said, "Follow me."

The two boldly worked their way up to the house with suppressive fire. After knocking down the front door, they shot at insurgents who fled toward the back of the house. Containing the enemy allowed other Marines to reach their fallen comrades and pull them out of the danger zone. By then, the sergeant who had been knocked out regained his senses and helped rescue the wounded.

A second fire team of Corporal Joseph Thomas, Lance Corporal Sajjad Rizvi, Lance Corporal Aaron Reynolds, and Sergeant Andrew Taylor came in behind Goodwin and Camp after the two had cleared the two front rooms. Reynolds and Rizvi went up the stairs while Taylor and Thomas cleared the left back room. Goodwin and Camp stalked down the hallway and came to a mini closet under the staircase. It looked too small to hold anyone with a weapon. "I have a sneaky suspicion that someone is in there," Camp whispered. "Should we throw a grenade?"

Goodwin shook his head. "Shrapnel could hit us."

Just to be safe, Camp fired several rounds into the closet. *That should have killed anyone in there,* he thought.

Taylor and Thomas announced they had cleared the back room. As Camp and Goodwin stepped out the back door, Lance Corporal Richard Cain was on the roof of a neighboring house and shot at insurgents who were poised to ambush the two in the back courtyard. Other Marines with Cain finished off some of the militants who had been flushed out of the house. However, one of the wounded insurgents was still alive and crawled behind cover in a corner. With his dying breath, the bleeding fanatic aimed his AK-47 at Camp, but Goodwin wheeled around and shot and killed him.

*I hope my luck holds out,* Camp thought.

"Let's check the house again," said Goodwin. Camp was walking into the back doorway when Goodwin, who was 10 feet in front of him, opened the little closet door under the stairwell. Suddenly automatic gunfire erupted, and Goodwin toppled to the floor from multiple gunshot wounds to his head. But he was still alive.

*Oh, no! They got him.* Camp was filled with rage, but fought the urge to charge down the hall, firing his weapon. *I can't just run in there, or we'll both be dead. And then two more Marines will be forced to risk their lives to drag out our bodies. The only way to get him out is to kill them first.*

Camp crept up as far as he could without being exposed and whispered to Goodwin, "Where are they? In the closet or down the hallway? Can you point to them?"

His face drenched in blood, Goodwin couldn't talk. But with great effort, he raised his quivering hand and then dropped it without making clear where the bullets were coming from.

Camp inched closer to Goodwin, hoping to drag him out. But Camp encountered a surprising amount of enemy rounds, which forced him to roll out the back door. The insurgents' bullets were bursting right through the cement walls, but his ammo wasn't able to penetrate them. *They're using armor-piercing rounds!*

Nevertheless, Camp was determined to get Goodwin out, so he crawled back into the house. He narrowly dodged militants' rounds while avoiding some of his own that ricocheted off the concrete. When Camp neared Goodwin, his heart sank. The sergeant was dead. *Nooo!* Before Camp could pull the body out of the house, machine-gunfire erupted. He and other Marines found themselves pinned under a barrage of enemy bullets from several directions.

The leathernecks fought back in a pitched battle that went on for hours. The militants blasted away at Camp, who was in the back courtyard, and other Marines who tried storming the house. But the leathernecks were repelled, and two more were wounded. Camp had never been this frightened in his life, but he persevered. *Where should I go to kill these guys?* he wondered. *What's the best angle of attack? How can I get to them?*

It became painfully obvious that the insurgents were using Goodwin's body, which was lying in front of the closet by the back room doorway, to draw the Marines into a trap. Two militants hiding in a bunker under the wood floor in front of the closet were blindly firing machine guns in a 180-degree arc up through the floorboards whenever anyone approached.

Rather than risk more lives, the Marines brought in a tank and watched it fire seven rounds into the house. *Well, if there were anyone in there, they're surely dead,* Camp thought. Just in case, he trained his weapon on a large hole in the side of the wall, giving him a clear view of the mini closet door, which was now closed. Several Marines rushed in. But when Lance Corporal Scott Bunker opened the closet door, he discovered an insurgent was in a hole in the back of the closet with just his machine gun exposed above the floor.

Reacting quickly, Bunker ripped off a few rounds before he was struck by enemy bullets twice in his left arm and once in his left lung. Another round broke off a piece of his rifle, which slammed into his face and took out his right eye. He collapsed. Before the militants could finish him off, Lance Corporal Nicholas Erdy crawled over to Bunker and dragged him to safety as rounds whizzed above their heads.

"The enemy came here to die," Hurley told his fellow Marines. "They're willing to stay in place and die with no hope. All they want is to take us with them. That's not going to happen."

Camp and his fellow leathernecks fought through the night using night-vision goggles. It took 12 hours and five assaults by the Marines — plus grenades, a bombing run by an F/A-18 attack plane, tank rounds, and rocket fire — to kill all the insurgents. At the end of the exhausting battle, Derga and Goodwin were dead and at least six more of the company's Marines were badly wounded and had to be medevaced out.

The fact that Camp wasn't injured was little consolation to him. He and his comrades were grieving over the two deaths — the first fatal casualties in their unit. Camp had looked up to

Goodwin and considered him a superb leader. Everyone was going to miss him and Derga, too. Derga was the squad's practical joker, the guy who kept everyone loose. He had planned on becoming a fireman after his tour of duty ended.

It was by far the most ferocious and intense firefight that the company had waged since arriving in Iraq. One of the Marines who was most shaken by the casualties was Christopher Dixon. He talked to Camp at length, sharing his feelings about fear and death. "We're all scared," Camp told him. "But we did what we had to do. So did you. You can't let yourself get down, okay? You'll be all right. We all will."

The next day, the military command gave the men of Lima Company light duty away from the action so they could regroup mentally and emotionally. But then Camp and his fellow leathernecks continued their gritty role in Operation Matador only to face the ghastly pain and suffering of May 11.

The deadly IED that blew up the amtrac killed or wounded the rest of the battle-ready members of his squad. In fact, the squad simply ceased to exist. In addition to Christopher Dixon, five other Marines died in the blast:

* Staff Sergeant Kendall H. Ivy, 28, who had just joined the unit, replacing Goodwin. He left behind a pregnant wife and three children.

* Lance Corporal Wesley G. Davids, 20, who died on his birthday.

* Lance Corporal Nicholas B. Erdy, 21, whose grandmother received a letter from him on the day she learned of his death. He had written her that he was safe and "not to worry too much."

* Lance Corporal Jonathan W. Grant, 23, who left behind two children.

* Lance Corporal Jourdan L. Grez, 24, who had joined the Marines because he wanted his two-year-old son, Colin, to be proud of him.

Camp was taken from the battlefield in a helicopter and flown to a hospital in Germany, where he was treated for second-degree burns on his face and third-degree burns on his hands. At first, doctors thought they might have to amputate his right hand because severe swelling was cutting off the blood supply. But they were able to save it. He remained in the hospital for three weeks while undergoing several skin grafts and recovering from shrapnel wounds in his legs and abdomen.

The fragment from the grenade missed severing a major artery in his leg by two inches and left a nine-inch scar. It made Camp realize how close he had come to dying and left him believing that he was spared for a reason other than chance. He couldn't walk, even at a shuffle, for three weeks and couldn't tie his shoes for three months.

The war continued to take its toll on Lima Company. A few months after the leathernecks' deaths during Operation Matador, the unit was further devastated when three antitank mines stacked on top of each other and buried under the road blew up a 25-ton personnel carrier, killing 14 Marines. Sniper fire and ambushes days before and after the tragedy claimed even more lives. By the end of its seven-month tour, almost a third of the company had been killed or wounded. In all, 59 Purple Hearts were given to Lima's casualties, 23 posthumously (after they died).

The company is no longer called Lucky Lima. If anything, it's the unluckiest unit of all because no combat unit in the Iraq War has suffered more casualties during a single deployment. In fact, no combat unit has sacrificed more.

*Lance Corporal Mark Camp, 25, received the Silver Star during a ceremony in Columbus, Ohio, in 2006. He earned the medal for his dramatic rescue attempts on May 11, 2005, and for repeatedly attacking the enemy during the deadly firefight three days earlier.*

*Recovered from his wounds yet bearing the scars of war, Camp graduated from college and married his girlfriend, Maria.*

# Courage
# in the
# Kill Zone

## HOSPITAL CORPSMAN THIRD CLASS
## JOSHUA CHIARINI

It was Hospital Corpsman Joshua Chiarini's second day in country. He stood in line at the mess hall of a U.S. Army base in Iskandaria, Iraq, which was about to be turned over to the Marines. He was talking to a gunnery sergeant about the brief firefight with insurgents that had taken place the night before.

"That was pretty exciting," Chiarini told him. "I'm glad nobody got hurt."

Suddenly, a large explosion that reminded him of a deafening crack of thunder rocked the other side of the large mess hall. A second blast shook the building as soldiers screamed in pain while others ran in all directions. More explosions ripped into the hall, including one that blew out the wall behind Chiarini.

"What's going on?" he asked.

"We're getting mortared!" yelled the gunny.

"I need to get my med bag now!"

"Follow me!"

They sprinted out of the mess hall, dived into a Humvee, and roared across the sprawling base. Their vehicle, however, didn't escape the attention of the enemy. To the left and right of the two Americans, mortar shells slammed into the ground, sending up geysers of dirt.

"They're trying to blow us up!" Chiarini shouted, his voice laced with fear. "Drive faster!"

When they reached his tent, Chiarini grabbed his medical supplies and jumped back into the Humvee for the perilous return ride. Dodging fresh craters and scrambling soldiers, the two reached an area where hundreds of tents were ablaze in a fast-moving firestorm.

Adding to the madness, weapons and ammo that soldiers had stored under their beds in the tent city were cooking off from the intense flames. Hand grenades, bullets, rockets, and mortar rounds were blowing up every second.

Chiarini rushed from one casualty to another, barking instructions to comrades who helped give basic first aid to the fallen. He leaped into the back of a parked ambulance to treat seriously injured victims and accompanied them to the medevac site. As he offloaded them, Chiarini looked up and saw Black Hawk helicopters lined up in the sky, waiting to land and take the wounded to a military trauma center. The injuries mounted up — 10, 20, 30. Four more were dead.

At one point during the chaos, the corpsman came across

a soldier who had suffered a serious blast wound to his arm and was wincing in agony. "I'm going to take care of you," Chiarini said, trying to calm him while stemming the bleeding. "Hey, everything's going to be okay. You're going to get a Purple Heart, and we're going to get you out of here. How does that sound?"

"Real good, man," the soldier said with a grimace. "I only have two weeks left. I almost made it without getting hurt. How long have you been here, Doc?"

"I got here yesterday."

The soldier shook his head and said, "Man, I feel real sorry for you."

Following in the footsteps of his grandfather — a 20-year navy veteran — Chiarini joined the U.S. Navy in 2000, three months after graduating from high school in his hometown of Coventry, Rhode Island. The teenager chose to be a corpsman because he enjoyed helping people.

Shortly after the invasion of Iraq, Chiarini volunteered for the first of his three tours of duty in the battle-battered country. He knew bad things were going to happen in combat and he wanted to be there when they did so he could save lives. But the job was hard, and it forced him to curb his emotions.

Assigned to the Marines, he lost a whole squad during his first month in country from combat injuries and IEDs. He was just getting to know many of his comrades when they fell. A mortar ripped off the legs of a fleeing leatherneck before he could reach a bunker. A fatal round blew out the throat of a Marine who days earlier had proudly announced he was going to be a dad for the first time. On Chiarini's birthday, his best friend in the platoon died when the Humvee he was riding in flipped over and crushed him.

The military couldn't get replacements fast enough, so his platoon operated with only two squads instead of the normal three. He once confided to a friend, "I have the mindset that I probably won't be coming home. If it's my time to go, then it's my time to go. This is my calling, and I'm okay with that." He received some comfort from his mother, who wrote him, "If you die over there or are seriously hurt, I can accept it because you're doing what you love."

Chiarini became close to his Marines, including his squad leader, Sergeant Jayton Patterson, who was respected and loved by his men. In the quiet times, the two talked about the important things in life and how much their families meant to them. And they talked about death; how you never know when your number is up; how luck sometimes chooses if you live or die.

"If I get killed, at least my wife will get the insurance money to pay off our SUV," Patterson once joked.

"Don't talk like that," Chiarini cautioned.

In Iraq, the enemy often receives a bonus for killing a medical person because it would deflate the fighting morale and spirit of the Americans. That's why corpsmen don't wear special insignias during combat. Chiarini blended in with the rest of the grunts, choosing to carry an M16 rifle and a pistol. He fought in combat until he was needed to treat a wounded Marine, at which time he used his weapons to protect his patient.

One of the most dangerous assignments for the platoon was walking along the road, looking for IEDs, usually artillery shells that the insurgents had rigged up and placed in holes. During a patrol, the Marines, including Chiarini, took turns walking point — being the lead person in a line. One day, he was the point man when the blasting cap of an IED next to him went off, sending dirt into his face. But, miraculously, it didn't set off the bomb. "Man, I should be in a thousand pieces by now," he told Patterson. "I got lucky today."

Later Chiarini was sitting at a patrol base taking a nap when he heard an explosion a couple of miles away. *Another IED,* he told himself. He fell back to sleep but was soon awakened by a Marine who blurted, "Patterson just got blown to bits."

Chiarini felt like he had fallen off a cliff. He couldn't move. "What happened?"

"We were out on an IED sweep. He looked in the hole, then back at us, and . . . *boom!* He was vaporized in an instant."

The corpsman was too numb to say anything or even cry. Instead, he went to the site of the blast and stared at the gaping hole by the side of the road. A hundred yards away, searchers had found Patterson's helmet and 200 yards in the opposite direction was his flak jacket. Chiarini joined in the search to pick up his friend's possessions and found Patterson's gloves, which had been turned inside out from the blast, and his name tape. The sergeant's death left the corpsman feeling empty and overwhelmed with grief.

The times Chiarini thought about his mortality the most came after he and part of his platoon were hunkered down in a patrol base about the size of a football field. The little base had two metal shipping containers large enough for the troops to sleep in and two more containers that held food and water.

Every day about noon, the enemy attacked the satellite base with mortar rounds. Chiarini could hear each mortar go off with a thump in the distance. And each time he wondered, *Do I have 30 seconds to live? Is this the day I die? Well, there's nothing I can do about it.* There were no bunkers for protection. All he could do was crouch and wait and wonder where the round would land. Unlike an RPG that whistles and flies horizontally, mortar rounds come in vertically and travel so fast that the sound trails the round. Whenever he heard incoming mortar — it sounds like a fast-moving train — he knew it was about to strike dangerously close. The hair on the back of his neck would stand up just before impact. If the blast force or shrapnel didn't kill anyone within a few feet, the explosion could suck the air out of their lungs. Those moments — waiting for the incoming — were the longest 30 seconds of Chiarini's life.

While on a patrol one day, Chiarini and his comrades pulled into a small palm grove and soon heard mortar rounds nearby. They drove into an open field where an insurgent loaded a mortar tube in his car and sped off. The Americans chased after him until they were intercepted by a truck carrying five insurgents who opened fire on them with AK-47s.

Chiarini and the Marines fought back. During the firefight, the machine gun on one of the Humvees malfunctioned, forcing the gunner to cock his weapon each time and fire one shot at a time. Then Chiarini's Humvee got stuck in the mud, so the platoon sergeant called in air support. Within minutes, Apache attack helicopters roared overhead.

The five militants leaped out of the truck and began to flee. Chiarini pursued one who climbed over a berm next to a canal and disappeared. When Chiarini reached the top of the berm, he scanned the area for the insurgent. *Where did he go? There's nothing but the canal and an open field in front of me. Why don't I see him?* Walking along the berm, Chiarini heard a splash behind him. He wheeled around and saw the militant surface from under the water, where he had been breathing through a hollow reed. The insurgent was planning to shoot the corpsman in the back, but Chiarini was too quick and aimed his M16 rifle at the enemy's heart.

His face contorted in fear, the bearded man, whose head was shaved, dropped his AK-47, threw his hands in the air, and pleaded in broken English, "No, mister! No, mister!"

Chiarini looked at the militant's wide, terror-stricken eyes and shaky hands. *He thinks I'm going to kill him right here,* the corpsman thought, *but he's worth much more to us alive than he is dead.* Chiarini smiled and shouted to his comrades, "I got him! I got him!" The other Marines rushed over and dragged the insurgent out of the water. As they led him away, the militant, who was grateful he wasn't killed, turned to Chiarini and said, "Thank you, mister."

Back at the base, the man gave up valuable information that led to the capture of several high-level enemy combatants and the discovery of a large weapons cache. For his actions, Chiarini was awarded the Navy Achievement Medal with Valor.

Later, while the platoon was out on a night patrol, a Humvee that was three vehicles ahead of Chiarini's was struck by an earsplitting, blinding explosion from an IED.

Chiarini leaped out and dashed toward the torn-up vehicle in the road. He could hear his Marines inside screaming in pain and yelling for him, "Corpsman up! Doc! Doc! We need you!"

Chiarini whipped open the back door and at first saw nothing but blood spilling out. He jumped inside to find four seriously wounded leathernecks. The legs of one were slashed so severely by shrapnel that the corpsman could see through them. A sergeant was sprawled on the floor, with a severe head wound and sliced up by shrapnel from head to toe. Chiarini thought the Marine was dead, but then discovered he was barely breathing. The corpsman opened the sergeant's eyelids and saw that an eye was blown out. *I keep finding more and more things wrong with him. I don't think he's going to make it, but I've got to try to save his life.*

Chiarini worked at a feverish pace to stabilize him while at the same time dealing with three other seriously wounded troops. Knowing that all his Marines had received some basic first-aid training, he enlisted the help of those who weren't too badly hurt. Tossing bandages to them, he belted out a stream of instructions: "Apply pressure to that arm! Wrap the wound on that guy's foot! Hold on to that severed pinkie until I can get to it! Take this morphine and inject it in his leg. Keep that guy comfortable and calm him down."

Scrambling from one patient to the next, Chiarini faced a Marine who was paralyzed from the waist down because shrapnel had cut into his spine. The corpsman didn't have a C-collar — a device to stabilize his neck — so he cut off the Marine's boots and put one on each side of the patient's head and taped them to his skull to keep his head still.

Next, the corpsman worked on a lance corporal who had a penetrating head wound from a piece of shrapnel that was lodged in his skull. "I'm in so much pain," the victim moaned. "Doc, give me morphine. Please, Doc."

"I can't," Chiarini replied. "I can't use morphine on patients with head wounds because it causes the brain to swell. It'll kill you."

The lance corporal started to slur his words, and he drifted in and out of consciousness.

"Call for air medevac now!" Chiarini hollered to his radioman.

Forty-five minutes later, two CH–53 helicopters landed on the road, and members of a surgeon team bolted out and raced to the Humvee. "What do you need?" one of them asked.

"A backboard for a spinal injury and three stretchers. Two C-collars for head wounds."

Minutes later, Chiarini watched the copters take off with the wounded. *I did all I could do for them*, he thought. His hands were still shaking, and his uniform was covered with other Marines' blood. *All that time, I wasn't thinking. I was just reacting as if by instinct. Thank God for all that training.* He walked away to be by himself and prayed that his patients would make it.

They all survived. The sergeant who was close to death with the severe head injury regained about 80 percent mental capacity but lost an eye and a finger. His buddy who had been paralyzed was able to walk again, and so was the comrade whose legs had been nearly severed. The lance corporal who had suffered a head wound underwent 10 surgeries before he was sent home.

Returning to Camp Lejeune, North Carolina, after his nine-month deployment, Chiarini bumped into the fourth Marine, whose nickname is Goose, at a welcome-home ceremony for the battalion. When Goose saw the corpsman, he hugged him and gushed, "You saved my life." Turning to others nearby, Goose announced, "Hey, everyone, this is the guy who saved my life!" Goose gave him another hug and said, "You're my buddy forever."

The homecoming ceremony was bittersweet for Chiarini. His unit — its numbers dwindled by casualties — marched in front of proud relatives. Although he was minutes away from a joyous reunion with his family, it was hard for him to walk in the march. He hurt for those Marines who weren't in formation because they had made the ultimate sacrifice. And he hurt for their loved ones who attended the ceremony but had no one of their own to welcome home.

He also felt sad because this was the last time he would see many of the buddies with whom he had grown tight after enduring countless life-and-death situations together. Some were discharged, and others were sent to different duty stations. And there were those like Chiarini who returned to Iraq because they wanted to do it all over again.

During Chiarini's second deployment, many of his missions took place in al-Anbar province, a hotbed of violence in early 2006. His unit — Battalion Landing Team, First Battalion, Second Marines, Twenty-second Marine Expeditionary Unit — was harassed by snipers and also small roadside IEDs near the city of Ar Ramadi.

On the morning of February 10, 2006, Chiarini was riding shotgun in the third of a four-vehicle convoy sent out to do a routine IED sweep, checking the road for hidden bombs. Chiarini's group was one of more than a dozen out that day hunting down insurgents and protecting supply roads through the region.

About 11 A.M., on a stretch of road considered extremely dangerous near the village of Hit, he heard a loud boom near the lead Humvee. He could tell from the sound that it was a small explosion. But he was too far back to see exactly what was happening, because of the smoke.

Turning to his driver, Chiarini said, "Let's go check it out and make sure they're all right."

The front vehicle, which carried four Marines and an Iraqi-American interpreter named Kenny, had encountered an IED but sped out of the kill zone. A hundred yards away, they stopped and ran out to take up defensive positions while the gunner stayed in the turret to provide cover fire. From several hundred yards away, Chiarini saw them get out and tried to contact them by radio without success. "Hurry," he urged his driver.

As his vehicle moved closer, a much larger explosion tore into the men of the first Humvee. Two 155-mm artillery shells hidden in a sandbag discharged deadly shrapnel through the air, slicing into them.

"Oh, my God!" Chiarini shouted. "It looks like everyone got wiped out!"

"I can't believe what I just saw," muttered the driver, a Marine who had recently arrived in country.

Then insurgents, watching from a cluster of buildings about 400 yards away, began shooting at the Marines. But Chiarini couldn't tell what was happening, because the scene ahead was blotted out by dense smoke, and he couldn't hear above the din of gunfire and exploding hand grenades. He threw down his radio handset. "Let's go!" he ordered his driver.

But the young driver was so stunned by what he had witnessed that he froze at the wheel.

"I can't wait any longer," shouted Chiarini. "I need to save my Marines!"

Clutching his med bag, he leaped out of the Humvee and sprinted forward. His pockets were already stuffed with bleeder packs — bandages that help stem bleeding. He didn't bother taking his M16 rifle. *I probably won't make it that far anyway before I get shot,* he told himself. *And if I'm lucky enough to reach them, I'll be too busy to use my weapon.* As he raced toward the Marines, he saw dirt kicking up near his feet. *They're shooting at me. Run faster!*

When he reached the leathernecks, he saw they all had suffered shrapnel wounds to their arms, legs, and faces, some more severe than the others. He also realized that the militants were shooting at them from three directions.

The driver, who was temporarily blinded from the flash of the blast, was firing wildly toward the wrong side of the road. He had shrapnel wounds from head to toe, but none of the wounds were near vital organs, because his flak jacket had saved his life.

"You're shooting in the wrong direction!" Chiarini said. The corpsman turned him around and had him spray his rounds toward the main core of the insurgents.

The squad leader, who had suffered a bad arm injury, was screaming, "Kenny's arm is blown off! His arm is gone!"

"Calm down," Chiarini shouted back. The corpsman quickly assessed the Marines' injuries to see who needed treatment first. It was obvious that Kenny, stumbling around in complete shock while holding what was left of his arm, was hurt the worst.

"Kenny," said Chiarini. "Look at me. I'm going to take care of you."

Kenny, a middle-aged Iraqi-born man who had lived in Michigan, stared at the corpsman without saying a word. His severely wounded arm was hanging by just a piece of skin. Chiarini didn't show any facial expressions of shock or worry, because he knew patients could read the faces of medical personnel. *If he sees my eyes get big, he'll panic,* Chiarini thought.

One of the Marines was pointing to Kenny and yelling, "My God, his arm!"

"Shut up!" Chiarini barked. "You'll get Kenny crazed."

"Is my arm still there?" the interpreter asked.

"There's still some of it left," replied Chiarini. "I'm going to fix you up."

The corpsman wrapped what was left of Kenny's arm and stopped the bleeding. Meanwhile, the insurgents continued to fire on him and the leathernecks. Chiarini picked a rifle off the ground and fired back while still treating the interpreter. Then, with one arm, he held Kenny and with the other, he laid down suppressive fire as he hustled him across an open space of about 100 yards toward the second Humvee.

In the back of the vehicle, Chiarini continued to work on Kenny. Once the injury was stabilized, the corpsman jumped out and, while dodging bullets and shooting on the run, sprinted back to the first Humvee to treat the next most injured Marine.

A leatherneck had been hit in the back of the leg. Despite being wounded, he continued to fire back at the insurgents and killed the trigger man. (They would later learn that the person who set off the IED was a boy only 12 years old.) Chiarini patched up the Marine's wound and, while firing at the enemy, brought him safely to the second Humvee.

Chiarini returned to treat the squad leader's forearm. As Marines from the rest of the convoy joined the firefight, the corpsman led the wounded squad leader to the second vehicle. He did the same for the driver who had suffered a sizable hole in his left foot. Chiarini took the leatherneck's boot off and stabilized the injury.

A Marine quick-reaction force arrived from a nearby base with more corpsmen to help care for the wounded troops. Turning his patients over to the medical team, Chiarini grabbed his rifle again and joined the others in unleashing fire at the enemy forces until the battle ended and the insurgents were killed.

While riding back to the base, Chiarini relived in his mind those hectic, dangerous minutes. He recalled that during the heat of battle, he had a reassuring, confident feeling as though the courageous corpsmen who had served in previous wars were there by his side. *It's remarkable*, he thought. *I could feel their hands on my shoulders as I worked.*

The Marines he treated that day survived. Kenny lost his arm, but after he recovered from surgery, he returned to help the Americans, explaining, "I don't need an arm to be an interpreter."

Chiarini later ran into one of the drivers he saved that day. What the driver told him meant so much to the proud corpsman. "Doc," said the leatherneck, "I knew everything was going to be okay the moment I saw you come through the smoke."

*During his three tours of duty in Iraq, Hospital Corpsman Third Class Joshua Chiarini fought in at least 20 firefights and rode in 30 convoys that were hit by roadside bombs and another 3 by suicide bombers. He treated more than 100 wounded Marines without having any die at the scene.*

*On October 22, 2007, Chiarini was awarded the Silver Star for his lifesaving actions in combat outside the Iraqi village of Hit. "He reacted the way he did for one simple reason: to take care of the Marine at his right and the Marine to his left," Brigadier General David Berger, Second Marine Division's assistant division commander, said during the ceremony. "He would not let his fellow warriors down. He used himself to protect his comrades. We cannot ask anything more."*

# Crisis
# in the Sky

## CHIEF WARRANT OFFICER LORI HILL

**A**rmy Chief Warrant Officer Lori Hill was proud to fly the OH-58D Kiowa (rhymes with Iowa) Warrior helicopter in Iraq, even though it's considered the underdog of military aviation.

The tiny two-seater has none of the glamour of the bigger, more powerful attack helos (helicopters) such as the Apaches or Black Hawks. It doesn't command much respect from pilots of other aircraft, who note that the low-powered chopper is based on a civilian model often used by TV stations.

They also point out that its weapons don't swivel. The Kiowa's .50-caliber machine gun and seven rockets have to be aimed by relying on the same technique used nearly a century ago by the pilots of biplanes during World War I — point the aircraft at what you're trying to hit, fly directly at it, and shoot.

The copter doesn't even have a gun sight unless a pilot slashes an X onto the windscreen with a grease pencil.

Kiowa pilots fly without any doors, so they can see better out the sides. Of course, that also means less protection. Each crew member wears body armor and sits over an armor panel, but there's little else to shield him or her. The chopper has less armor than most any other military aircraft. To put more armor on the craft would force the crew to carry less fuel and ammunition to offset the added weight. So it remains the "small fry" of the army.

But the troops on the ground in Iraq have loved the "little helo that could." Like other pilots of the Kiowa, Hill protected infantry troops by darting above them, kept an eye out for threats ahead of them, and fought off insurgents by firing her guns and rockets. And that meant she had to bring her chopper close to the ground — and the enemy.

Hill was like a low-flying police officer, patrolling day and night in a dangerous area that could, and did, erupt into violence at any given moment.

During the first six months of her deployment in Iraq in 2005 and 2006 with the Second Squadron Seventeenth Calvary Regiment, the spunky redheaded pilot had been fired on a few times by insurgents but was never hit. Attached to the Apache helicopter battalion at a base in the city of Balad, Hill and her fellow pilots went out in pairs of Kiowas to scout ahead, conduct reconnaissance surveillance, provide convoy security, and respond to trouble.

When she climbed into her Kiowa at 3 A.M. on March 21, 2006, the 35-year-old pilot figured it would be another routine day. She and her copilot for the mission, Lieutenant Kevin White, followed the lead helo flown by Chief Warrant Officers Mike Slebodnik, pilot, and Mariko Kraft, copilot. Wearing night-vision goggles, the two crews provided overhead cover for two Bradleys that were patrolling two main roads in and out of the city of Muqdadiyah.

While eyeballing the horizon for anything suspicious, Hill couldn't help but look forward to the next day. That's when her squadron was scheduled to relocate to the Iraqi city of Kirkuk, where she would reunite with her husband, Dennis, also a Kiowa pilot, who was stationed there.

Around 6 A.M., the two choppers left the Bradleys alone to refuel at Forward Operating Base Normandy and then rejoin them. As the Kiowas were gassing up, Hill heard a radio call that the Bradleys were taking fire in Muqdadiyah near the Joint Command Center (JCC), the hub of operations in the area involving American troops, Iraqi soldiers, and Iraqi police.

The copter crews jumped into their aircraft and whizzed across the landscape at an altitude of only 35 feet to come to their aid. Soon Hill saw tracer fire aiming at the lead helo followed by an RPG. Slebodnik took immediate evasive action and wasn't hit. Seeing the rounds coming from a tree line, Hill fearlessly turned toward the trees to draw enemy fire away from the lead chopper so it could escape. After maneuvering to avoid RPGs, she laid down suppressive fire. To shoot her .50-caliber machine gun, she had to fly in straight at the insurgents while her copilot made sure all of the aircraft's systems were working properly.

As soon as Hill stopped attacking and broke away, the enemy started shooting at her chopper, so Slebodnik circled back and fired at them. At least three RPGs and untold number of machine-gun rounds were shot at Hill's aircraft. She expertly dodged the rockets while hearing the loud plinks from bullets striking the Kiowa.

It was the first time Hill had been in such a perilous situation. She had shot at gunnery ranges and trained for battle, but nothing could fully prepare her for actual combat, not when she was trying to shoot the enemy while they were trying to shoot her down. With an eye on the militants' tracer bullets, she continued to let loose with her .50-caliber until she was sure that the lead helo was safe.

"We need to bypass these guys and get to the Bradleys, because they're in trouble," said Lieutenant White. "We must protect them and the JCC."

The two choppers veered out of enemy range and continued on their way. Both pilots checked their instruments to make sure their crafts weren't damaged. The two multifunction displays (TV-like monitors called MFDs) had gone blank on Hill's chopper and no longer showed information such as altitude, airspeed, and visuals from an outside camera. She was forced to fly using standby instruments.

"We're good. We're good," Hill radioed Slebodnik. "We lost our MFDs, but everything else seems to be working okay, so let's keep going." She figured some bullets had struck the monitors' wiring that ran under White's armored seat. But as they flew on, she got a lucky break — the MFDs came back to life.

The choppers reestablished contact with the Bradleys, but

neither helicopter crew could see the vehicles at first because of the smoke from combat. The fliers didn't want to enter the fray without knowing the exact locations of the good guys and bad guys.

"We're gonna go in a little high." Slebodnik radioed Hill. "We need to get a better picture of what's going on below."

"Okay," she replied. "We'll stay low and cover you guys." She knew that the maneuver Slebodnik was making was a risky one, because it made his chopper more visible by hovering above the fighting. His Kiowa was like a sitting duck for any kind of machine-gunfire or an RPG. But it was the best way to assess the situation and find out exactly where the Bradleys were.

Through a break in the smoke, she spotted the Bradleys. What she had thought would be a small skirmish had turned into a much bigger battle. About 100 insurgents armed with AK-47s, belt-fed machine guns, IEDs, RPGs, and grenades were attacking the JCC. They also had pinned the Bradleys so the troops inside couldn't get to the command center to help out. Making things more difficult, several IEDs had exploded in front of the vehicles.

When the choppers closed in on the JCC, the entire sky lit up with machine-gun tracer rounds. "We're taking fire!" Slebodnik reported. With total disregard for her safety, Hill again maneuvered her aircraft to protect the lead helo. She put the nose down, and her helicopter hurtled out of the sky, spewing suppressive fire as Slebodnik banked away. Then she, too, broke off and circled around for another attack.

Like before, Hill had to turn and face enemy fire in order to shoot back. She couldn't worry that bullets might come crashing through the windshield at any moment. Putting the nose of her chopper down in order to fire her machine gun, she ripped off bursts for only a few seconds before she had to pull up to avoid crashing into the ground. Because the fight was being waged in the city, neither chopper shot any rockets, out of concern for risking the lives of innocent citizens or accidentally striking the JCC or any nearby houses. Although rockets would be more damaging than machine guns, they would have been less accurate, because the pilots didn't have enough time to aim and shoot them with precision.

In the face of concentrated enemy fire, Hill continued to engage the enemy with close combat attacks from various directions and at heights as low as 20 feet. Her courageous efforts allowed the troops in the Bradleys to get unpinned and unleash their own firepower as they fought their way toward the JCC. Once she finished shooting, she yanked hard right and yanked hard left, changing her altitude so she wouldn't become such an easy target.

On the next pass, the sky lit up again with enemy fire. Slebodnik shot off several rounds before Hill brought her chopper in and fired, suppressing the insurgents' guns so that the troops on the ground could scurry to better positions.

Then she did a hard right break, leaving the entire belly of her craft exposed to enemy fire for a few seconds. As she talked on the radio to Slebodnik, she heard bullets slamming into her chopper.

Suddenly, she was jolted by a sharp pain in the bottom of her right heel and up through her ankle. It felt as if her foot had been struck by a hardball hurled at 100 miles an hour.

"Owww!" she groaned.

"Lori, are you okay?" Slebodnik asked.

"Yeah, I guess so. My ankle is stinging, that's all."

She wasn't sure what had happened to her. She looked down at her foot and didn't see anything unusual, although she was in a lot of pain. "I think a piece of metal flew off the aircraft and hit my ankle really hard." *I can't worry about how bad it hurts,* she told herself. *The guys on the ground need us right now.*

"Ready for another pass?" Slebodnik radioed.

"Yep, let's do it," Hill replied.

They flew in several circles before making the next assault on the insurgents. As the choppers broke off, Slebodnik radioed, "We took some hits. We're slowly losing transmission pressure."

Hill looked at the display on her control panel and tensed up. "Hey, ours is completely gone," she reported. Hill knew that without the fluid, the chopper's transmission would eventually seize, and the craft would fall out of the sky. *Hope what I read in the manual is true that this craft will fly for up to 30 minutes without transmission fluid.* She figured she had a decent chance of landing safely, because Forward Operating Base Normandy was about 20 minutes away.

"We need to get back to Normandy now," she told Slebodnik. The pain in her foot was getting worse, so when they headed back, she transferred control of the chopper to her copilot, Lieutenant White, and then looked at her boot again. But she still couldn't tell what had happened to her.

"Hey, Lori," said White, "I think we're losing our hydraulics."

She took back the controls. The helo hardly responded to her, making it difficult to fly. "Oh, yeah, they're definitely gone," she said. Flying a chopper without hydraulics is like driving a car without any power steering, only much harder.

*Well, this is interesting,* she thought. *We have no transmission pressure and no hydraulics. There's nothing I can do about the transmission, but there is something I can do to compensate for the hydraulics.* It required some slick flying skills and a lot of muscle from the five-foot four-inch, 125-pound Hill and her five-foot six-inch, 135-pound copilot to operate the controls.

There was another problem. Without hydraulics, the chopper couldn't hover as it made its approach to land. Instead, Hill would have to do a run-on landing, in which the helo would come in horizontal to the ground, like a fixed wing aircraft, and then skid to a stop.

"We're going to do a run-on landing at Normandy," she radioed Slebodnik.

"Hey, Lori, are you sure you can do it?"

"Dude, I don't have much choice."

"Okay, I'll go ahead to make sure everything is clear. Everything's gonna be okay. Remember to stay low and slow."

"Yep, I'll see you back there."

Looking for any advantage, Hill fingered the one lucky charm that she always carried with her — her husband's dog tag. For good luck, the couple had given each other their extra dog tag after they had been deployed to Iraq. She couldn't wait to see Dennis again.

*My, how my life has taken some unexpected turns,* she thought.

Born and raised in Springfield, Oregon, Hill (whose maiden name is Kiefer) joined the army at age 17 fresh out of high school. She planned to serve for two years and use the money she earned to attend college. But she ended up reenlisting so she could go to Germany and see the world. Hill became a supply sergeant with a signal unit that was deployed to Iraq during the first Persian Gulf War. Later, while pondering her future, she had to make a decision: either leave the military or try something new in the army. An aptitude test indicated she would make a good helicopter pilot, so she tried it even though she had never touched a helo in her life. At flight school, she fell in love with flying — and also with fellow chopper pilot Dennis Hill. They wed at Fort Campbell, Kentucky, in 2004. Because they were in the same squadron, they were deployed to Iraq at the same time, but they weren't allowed to fly together.

*I can't wait to see him tomorrow,* she thought, wishing the stricken Kiowa was already safely on the ground.

Spotting two other Bradleys on a long dirt road, Hill radioed to Slebodnik, who was flying ahead of her, "If I can't make it to Normandy, I can try landing on the road."

"We'll make sure the road is clear in case you need it," he told her. "If you go down, we'll be there for you, but, knowing you, I'm sure you can make it back."

Hill appreciated his confidence in her. She chose not to think about when the transmission would start to shred itself and send the chopper plunging toward earth. Instead, she looked for the positives of her situation. *The blades are still turning, and the engine is still running,* she thought.

Normandy was in sight. Her biggest worry now was to land without skidding into the Hesco barriers (sand-filled containers of wire mesh and heavy-duty plastic used to protect against small-arms fire) that surrounded the helipad. *If I don't do this right, we'll smash right into the Hescos,* she thought.

"We're going to go in real low and slow," she told her copilot. "It might be rough, but we can do this."

Gripping the controls with all their might, Hill and White held their breath as the Kiowa balked at responding to their efforts on the controls. Losing altitude, the helo barely cleared the Hesco at the end of the helipad. When the skids touched the ground, the chopper slid and bounced for about 10 feet before coming to a stop for a picture perfect run-on landing. Hill turned to White and grinned. "Nice job, sir."

"Nice job, Lori."

They gave each other a high five.

Hill went ahead with the emergency shutdown and then told White, "Stay here until the blades stop. I'm getting out to check on my ankle."

She limped away from the chopper and then sat down on the ground and yanked off her boot. Blood poured out. *Oh, oh, this isn't good,* she thought. She peeled off her soaked sock and saw blood running out of a hole in her ankle. Bits of bone fragment were visible. "Hey, sir," she yelled to White. "I think I'm going to need a medic."

"What's wrong, Lori?"

"I'm not sure, but I think I got shot."

When the medic arrived, he took one look at the ankle and said, "Yep, you've been shot all right."

Hovering over her were Slebodnik and Kraft. Joked Slebodnik, "You got shot! That's so cool! You're the first in our troop to take a round. Do you have a camera?" After she told him where it was, he got it and took several pictures of her wound and also her shot-up helicopter.

"If I had been walking down the street and been shot in the ankle, I probably would have passed out, but the adrenaline had kicked in during the fight," Hill told her comrades. "I didn't pay attention to my foot because I had a job to do."

She was medevaced to a hospital in Balad, where doctors discovered the round had gone through the bottom of her heel and out the top of her ankle. It had broken her tibia (shin bone) in three places and shattered her ankle bone but didn't damage the tendons. The doctors told her the wound was serious enough to require treatment in Germany. Hill begged them to let her go with her troop to Kirkuk so she could be with her husband, but it wasn't possible. Her only consolation was that Dennis flew from Kirkuk to Balad to see her for a few hours.

As a going-away present, Slebodnik brought Hill her hand-held GPS that had been in the side windshield next to her seat. Embedded in the device was the enemy .762 round that had gone through her foot, out her ankle, through a compass-card holder, and into the GPS. She dug the round out of the GPS and kept it as a souvenir.

Her fellow pilots counted 25 bullet holes in her craft, some under the copilot's seat. At least eight rounds had hit above their heads in the engine cowling right below the blades. "We were lucky none came in through our windscreen or we would have been shot," she told her comrades.

Hill was most proud and gratified to learn that the JCC was saved and that the troops in the Bradleys were safe. In fact, the only American injured that day was Hill.

Her flight was the last one she ever flew for the army. She remained in a cast for two and a half months and then underwent weeks more of physical therapy. By the time she was medically cleared to fly again, her unit had returned from Iraq. After having served 20 years, she retired from the army and began a new and, in some ways, more challenging career — as a full-time mom.

*On October 16, 2006, Vice President Dick Cheney flew to Fort Campbell, Kentucky, and awarded Chief Warrant Officer Lori Hill the Distinguished Flying Cross for her heroics of seven months earlier. The citation noted that instead of focusing on her injury or the airworthiness of her helicopter, she drew fire away from the lead aircraft, established communication with the soldiers on the ground, and suppressed fire so they could reach safety. She also received a Purple Heart.*

*Lieutenant Kevin White and Chief Warrant Officers Mike Slebodnik and Mariko Kraft were given Air Medals with Valor for their roles in the battle.*

*Recalling that day in March, Hill said, "I was glad I didn't pass out and very happy I was able to help the soldiers out and get our helicopter down safely on the ground." She added, "It's a little joke with everybody that on my last flight I went out with a bang."*

# "We Must Stand Our Ground"

## STAFF SERGEANT CHAD MALMBERG

**S**taff Sergeant Chad Malmberg was scared. The convoy of supply trucks that he was entrusted to protect was trapped with nowhere to go and under siege by a swarming band of well-armed militants, who outnumbered his 15-man security force by as many as 10 to 1. To make the situation even more frightening, his guys were running out of ammunition.

The fear Malmberg felt wasn't so much for his own safety — he was prepared to give his life if necessary — but for the safety of his soldiers and the civilian truck drivers. The split-second decisions he would have to make, the commands he would have to give, and the actions he would have to take all had to be dead right in order to beat back the assault.

Malmberg had never faced such a terrifying situation before, even though he was an experienced soldier and commander of a convoy-escort team. For the previous six months, he and his troops had shepherded semi trucks loaded with food, fuel, and supplies on grueling round trips in Iraq up to 608 miles long over three days. Sometimes one leg of the trip would take 20 hours to complete. They drove in heat, which soared up to 141 degrees Fahrenheit, and through all-penetrating sand that blew so thick no one could see past the hood. Adding to the misery, he and his men wore Kevlar vests, long sleeves, gloves, and gear that added another 50 to 60 pounds in the unbearable heat.

But those conditions were mere annoyances compared to the real threats to the convoys — roadside bombs, snipers, and ambushes. Whenever one of his convoys was attacked, it was usually by a small number of insurgents who were quickly mowed down by his accurate gunners, and the trucks kept rolling. Through it all, the 27-year-old staff sergeant always remained cool, giving orders with calm confidence. In fact, he was known to eat a sandwich during firefights, dishing out commands with a mouth full of food. (He has a high metabolism, which means he must eat frequently.)

As the number of his successfully led missions mounted over the months, Malmberg felt increasingly lucky — yet wary — because even though he rode in the scout truck about a half mile ahead of each convoy, his vehicle hadn't been struck by an IED. He knew it was bound to happen someday. He just didn't know when.

One foggy night while he was riding in his scout truck, a heavily armored Humvee, the headlights cast a dim glow on a pile of broken asphalt. Spotting detonation cord snaking out from the rubble, he shouted, "IED!" The driver, Specialist Edward Scullion, slammed on the brakes a second before the bomb exploded a few feet in front of the vehicle. The blast stunned Malmberg and Scullion and knocked the gunner, Specialist James Chastain, down from his perch in the turret. It cracked the windows — one piece of shrapnel was wedged in the windshield directly in front of Scullion's face — and broke the headlights, but did little other damage to the Humvee. Falling rock and debris pelted the truck while its three occupants checked themselves for injuries.

Malmberg couldn't help it. He laughed. Not because he thought it was funny, but because he gushed with relief. He had been on so many trips where IEDs had exploded ahead of his convoy or behind it. He had heard over the radio of dozens of other attacks. He had driven by huge craters caused by the roadside bombs. And all during that time, he had kept wondering, *When will my luck run out? When will it be my turn?* The nerve-racking anticipation had been building inside him for so long that when it finally happened to him, he thought, *So this is what it's like to get hit by an IED. It's not so bad — but that's because I'm in my armored truck.*

Malmberg stopped chortling when he looked back and saw that Chastain had the wind knocked out of him. "Are you all right?" Malmberg asked him. Covered in dust and debris from the explosion, Chastain coughed up smoke and mumbled, "Yeah." Malmberg, who could see fragments embedded in Chastain's ballistic goggles, felt bad for laughing, because the gunner had taken the brunt of the blast.

Malmberg's Humvee was still functioning, so the convoy pressed onward to its destination, just as all the others had done under his command as a member of A Company, Second Battalion, 135th Infantry.

The native of Saint Paul, Minnesota, had enlisted in the army right out of high school and trained as a paratrooper but was never deployed overseas. After completing three years of service, he joined the Minnesota Army National Guard's Thirty-fourth Infantry Division (nicknamed the Red Bulls) in 2001 and enrolled at Minnesota State University–Mankato. In 2005, when the West Saint Paul–based unit he had trained with was set to deploy to Iraq, he was offered a position as squad leader. Even though he was only a semester away from completing his bachelor's degree in law enforcement and could have finished school first, he couldn't resist the chance to serve with his buddies in the Red Bulls.

A few months after arriving in Iraq, Malmberg was made commander of a convoy-escort team. The trucks he and his men protected pushed through all the skirmishes and typical hit-and-run attacks ... until the fateful night of January 27, 2007.

He was in the scout truck with four other gun trucks spaced throughout a convoy of 20 flatbed semis. As they chugged down a six-lane highway south of Baghdad about 10:30 P.M., his eyes were glued to the road while his stomach was begging for the take-out box he got from the chow hall — a turkey sandwich, chips, beef jerky, and an apple. Suddenly, a few miles ahead of them, he saw flares and light flashes and heard a thunderous blast. An IED had exploded, forcing another convoy ahead of Malmberg's to screech to a halt. One of the 25 trucks in that group had been badly damaged, and debris blocked the road.

Malmberg's convoy stopped about a quarter mile away to wait while the route-clearing team could check for more IEDs on the road and a tow truck could remove the smoking wreckage. Knowing there was a strong likelihood that the enemy would attack, Malmberg positioned his gun trucks so they were in the best defensive position to protect his convoy.

Just as he expected, small-arms fire erupted, targeting the first convoy. On his orders, his vehicle and another gun truck sped over to help defend the first convoy while the rest of his team remained behind. He immediately began firing at several militants who were shooting from nearby berms and ditches. After about 10 minutes, the firefight quieted down. "I guess the enemy has had enough," he told his driver, Specialist Daniel Schwichtenberg. "They're either dead or they've fled." It appeared to be just another aggravating attack from a small group of insurgents.

Malmberg was giving himself a silent pat on the back for a job well done when Specialist Kyle Kosloske, commander of the fourth gun truck, which was in the rear of Malmberg's convoy, called on the radio and said, "Hey, we're receiving fire back here. We're engaging." Kosloske gave the estimated distance and direction of the enemy fire. Now Malmberg's convoy was part of this ambush. He thought, *Either there are two independent enemy groups, or else this is a coordinated attack that's spreading out.* This wasn't typical of the insurgents, and that made him uneasy.

Malmberg's gun truck and the other one that had followed him roared back to his convoy, where he repositioned his men to take on the enemy. The cool night was getting rattled by the sounds of AK-47s and RPGs. Within minutes, the militants were also targeting the front of Malmberg's convoy. At first, he estimated the enemy force had about 12 insurgents — one group toward the front and the other near the rear.

The area selected by the insurgents consisted of a well-defined kill zone with berms running parallel to the road at 100- to 200-meter intervals and canals running perpendicular, which gave them excellent cover. While under enemy small-arms fire, Malmberg dismounted his truck in an attempt to clear the road so his convoy could exit the kill zone. But it was impossible for the convoy to move forward — median rails separating the north- and southbound lanes prevented the big trucks from turning around. *This definitely isn't your run-of-the-mill engagement,* he told himself. *We must stay and fight. We must stand our ground.*

Over his headset he told his men to maintain their composure, explaining, "We need to defend until we can get out of here."

He coordinated the firing of his team's weapons, gave updated reports to other units on the ground, and called for air support. He paid no attention to the rounds from the AK-47s that were pinging and bouncing off his truck's armor.

Malmberg tried to count the muzzle flashes, but they were so far away, about 500 yards, he couldn't tell how many insurgents were attacking the convoy. He and his soldiers were waging the fight while wearing night-vision goggles so everything they saw through the lenses was in crisp, clear shades of green. It reminded him of when he used to play laser tag — except this time, the losers in this real-life game would die.

As the battle increased in ferocity and the rates of enemy fire picked up, Malmberg saw dozens of insurgents clad in dark outfits and black- and white-checkered head scarves. They were darting, crawling, and creeping from one berm to another, moving closer to the convoy. He realized he had greatly underestimated the size of the enemy and, for the first time, understood that he and his men were vastly outnumbered and in real danger of being overrun.

Malmberg knew he had to remain composed and collected while barking orders, because everybody in his group could hear everything that was being said on their headsets. *I'm the guy in charge, and if I sound like I'm freaking out, then they're likely to freak out, too*, he thought.

He was getting reports from the rear that one of the gun trucks was unable to take out a cluster of six enemy muzzle flashes. His men would shoot .50-caliber rounds and other small-arms fire at the position, but the moment they stopped firing, the militants would shoot back. *This doesn't make sense, unless they have some great cover*, he thought. *The only way to suppress them is to have constant bullets impacting the position, but we can't sustain that for a long time. I need to eliminate that target back there, because we can't keep this up all night.*

Malmberg rode to the rear of the convoy. After several

minutes of exchanging gunfire and unable to gain fire superiority, he told his team over his headset, "I want to end this right now. I'm going to fire the AT-four." The antitank rocket was the team's biggest weapon – one that he had never fired before in combat. In fact, he would be the first in the entire brigade to use the weapon during a battle. Getting a bead on the enemy position, he told Kosloske, "Have your gunner mark the target with tracer fire." Malmberg gave the same order to his own gunner. Then he prepped the AT4.

While under direct enemy fire, Malmberg jumped out of his Humvee and, using the hood of the truck as cover, locked in on the target. "Back-blast area clear!" he shouted, making sure no one was behind him, because the AT4 produces a fiery, powerful back blast.

He steadied his nerves and fired at the largest concentration of insurgents. Then he hustled back to the vehicle as the rocket slammed into the group of enemy shooters. Once inside the Humvee, Malmberg laughed from nervousness and excitement because he had hit the bull's-eye. He plugged his headset back in and reported, "AT-Four out!" He thought, *Wow, that was so cool!*

No more enemy fire came from that position. For a minute or two, the militants stopped shooting. "I think this fight is over," he told Schwichtenberg, his driver. "We'll sit here and wait to move out once the road is cleared." But no sooner had he spoken than the insurgents started firing at the convoy again, this time from much closer range.

*I can't believe that this is still going on*, Malmberg thought. Through his night-vision goggles, he saw insurgents fall and die, yet more kept advancing. He was trying to communicate with the first convoy through the radio, but too many people were talking. So three times he drove through a hail of bullets to the other convoy, got out, and traded information and tactics with its leaders. Their dangerous face-to-face meetings were brief because they were under intense enemy fire.

Ten minutes after he fired the AT4, the air support that he had requested arrived. Seeing two Apache attack helicopters hovering nearby, Malmberg felt hopeful that they would put an end to the battle. He directed his team to mark enemy positions with infrared lasers. But because of the intensity and chaos of the firefight, the two choppers couldn't help the units on the ground and flew off, dampening the spirits of the soldiers. Malmberg went from feeling "Yeah, they're here!" to "Oh, no, they're leaving!" *We're on our own,* he told himself. *This is going to be a long night.*

Over the next 35 minutes, he directed the actions of his gun trucks while continually moving his vehicle to the area of heaviest fighting. Seeing Malmberg in the thick of the firefight gave his comrades a big lift. "We're going to do whatever we have to do to win this thing," he told them.

If there was one thing he knew how to do, it was fight as the underdog. When he was a skinny kid, he learned how to box, and in competition he punched his way to one win after another. In the army, he became an expert in combatives — hand-to-hand fighting that combines elements of the martial arts, wrestling, and boxing. Even though he stood five foot nine and weighed 160 pounds, he held his own against opponents who were stronger and 60 to 100 pounds heavier than him. He was such a good fighter that he became a top instructor in combatives.

Malmberg discovered that in a tough fight he could function under stress, take a hit, and persevere. He learned how important it was to find the strengths and weaknesses of the opponent and of himself and to use that knowledge to his advantage. Now was the time — in this pitched battle where the odds were stacked against him and his team — for Malmberg to rely on his disciplined mindset and competitive heart.

His shoulders tensing from the strain, he knew his commands had to be perfect if he and his men were to survive this onslaught. Although time and again he exposed himself to danger, he was hoping he wouldn't get shot, because he didn't want to be a burden to his comrades. *I want to be a part of the solution, not a part of the problem,* he told himself.

The enemy was constantly popping up to the left and right, closing in on the Americans even though his gunners had been putting lead downrange at a furious rate for the sake of survival. As the battle raged, Malmberg worried that they would run out of ammunition. "Gunners, slow down your rate of fire," he ordered. "We need to conserve our resources." He knew there was no way they would get resupplied in time. The men whose trucks had the most ammo passed some of it to the others when they were under fire.

The militants were getting so close that he could see their faces from the illumination of the muzzle flashes from their weapons. He could hear their voices chattering and screaming in nearby ditches. "Make sure your doors are battle-locked," he told his men.

Busy directing the gun trucks and communicating with outside units, Malmberg didn't hear Kosloske in the fourth gun truck warn over the radio, "We're red [getting low] on ammo, and the enemy is fifty meters and closing." But a few seconds later, Malmberg heard Kosloske announce, "We're almost black [virtually out of] on ammo for the point-fifty-cal. We're transitioning [changing] to the M-Four. Now the enemy is twenty meters away."

*This is bad for us and smart for them,* Malmberg thought. *They were shooting from long range to keep us busy while another group was moving closer without us noticing. They're going to try and assault right through our fire to hijack the truck and maybe kidnap the crew.*

Immediately, he told Schwichtenberg, "Turn around and step on it!" In the headset, he told Kosloske, "We're on our way." Sergeant Christopher Oshea, who was in another gun truck, said, "We're coming, too." The two vehicles weaved around craters and passed the stalled semis as bullets bounced off the vehicles.

Told that 8 to 10 insurgents were behind the berm closest to Kosloske's gun truck, Malmberg began prepping a grenade. As soon as his Humvee stopped next to Kosloske's, Malmberg swung open his door and jumped out. Selflessly exposed to enemy fire, he hurled the grenade and yelled, "Frag out!" He had thrown a perfect strike. The grenade detonated right in the middle of the militants just as they were ready to storm the fourth gun truck.

Oshea's gunner Specialist Jason Jones then sprayed the area with his M240B machine gun. From his vantage point on the turret, Malmberg's gunner Specialist Robert Kenny shouted, "We killed them! We got 'em all!"

Malmberg had eliminated the main threat to the rear of his convoy. But he knew more insurgents were coming. Farther up, the second gun truck, commanded by Sergeant David Good and driven by Specialist Ryan Fossen, was in danger of being overrun by militants who were poised to charge out of a ditch from 20 yards away. Fossen backed up the Humvee just as a grenade exploded three feet in front of them. Fortunately, they weren't injured. Blake Romann, the gunner, wiped out the closest militants when he tossed several grenades into the ditch and then sprayed it with his M240B machine gun.

Malmberg was more determined than ever to lead the trucks out of the kill zone. He needed to find a path to get around the held-up convoy up front. Over the radio, he learned that an opening had been created. But before his semis could advance, the enemy launched a volley of 15 RPGs from about 150 yards out, first at the rear of the convoy and then working their way up the line toward the front, exploding ever closer to the semis and gun trucks.

Incredibly only one RPG found its mark, hitting the cab of a semi. Malmberg asked Kenny, "What do you see?"

"I think the RPG blew up the cab," his gunner replied. "Smoke is pouring out of both windows."

Assuming the driver was dead or seriously injured, Malmberg told Oshea, who was in the gun truck closest to the semi, "Go up there and secure the casualty."

Bullets were still flying. Oshea opened the door of the cab and was shocked when the driver jumped out and appeared to be uninjured. Oshea patted him down for wounds, but there wasn't a scratch on him.

The cab, however, was damaged. All the windows were blown out, and the door was charred. To see if the truck would run, Oshea climbed into the cab and started the engine. The semi was still operable. Then he stepped out and spotted the shaken driver hiding under the truck. The sergeant pulled him out and helped him back into the cab.

After taking more than 1,000 rounds and still being under fire, the convoy started to roll. When the trucks pulled out of the kill zone, Malmberg received reports on his headset from his team about injuries (none), damage to vehicles (minor), and amount of rounds left (not much). After everyone had reported in, he figured out that if the ambush had gone on another 10 or 15 minutes, he and his men would have exhausted all their ammo.

But thanks to his leadership and the accuracy of everyone in his team, at least 40 insurgents lay dead, and the rest of the enemy, despite being a larger force, had failed to overpower his convoy.

Guzzling a Gatorade from a cooler, Malmberg dipped into his to-go box for a stick of beef jerky. He leaned back in his seat and grinned. *No injuries, no real damage. Pretty awesome.* He thought back to the times when he was a kid and his dad would preach to him, "It's not the size of the dog in the fight that matters, but the size of the fight in the dog." Malmberg ripped off a hunk of jerky, took another big gulp of Gatorade, and thought, *Tonight we had a lot of fight in us.*

* * *

Nine months after the ferocious ambush of January 27, 2007, Staff Sergeant Chad Malmberg was awarded the Silver Star, becoming the first Minnesota Army National Guard member in his division to receive such a medal since World War II.

According to the citation, "Malmberg's gallant actions and determined leadership allowed his convoy, trapped in an enemy ambush for nearly fifty minutes, to dominate a numerically superior enemy fighting from prepared positions, without a single member of the convoy being wounded or killed in action, or loss of a single vehicle. His actions undoubtedly saved lives at great risk to his own."

# Glossary

**adrenaline:** a hormone produced by the body that prepares the individual to deal with stress

**AK-47:** an automatic assault rifle, originally manufactured in the former Soviet Union

**amtrac:** an amphibious assault vehicle that looks like an armored boat on tank tracks

**AT4:** a portable one-shot, antitank rocket launcher

**battalion:** a military unit usually consisting of from 500 to 1,500 persons in two to six companies and a head-quarters

**battle aid station (BAS):** a medical unit close to combat that treats the wounded before they are taken to a hospital

**berm:** a raised bank of earth, usually along a canal

**boots:** nickname given to new recruits in basic training, which is also known as boot camp

**Bradley:** an armored infantry fighting vehicle that looks like a tank and carries about nine soldiers

**cache:** a hiding place where weapons and ammunition are stored

**cammies:** slang for a uniform made from camouflage fabric

**casualty collection point (CCP):** a protected area for medical personnel to treat the wounded during combat

**combat lifesaver bag (CLS):** a bag with IV solution, bandages, and other items needed for first aid

**company:** a military unit usually consisting of three to five platoons

**cooking off:** ammunition exploding prematurely due to heat or fire

**corpsman:** a medically trained enlisted naval person assigned to provide battlefield medical care to Marines or sailors

**deployment:** the assignment of military personnel to a tour of duty

**firefight:** a battle between ground forces using guns, grenades, and other fired weapons

**fire team:** the smallest unit of the infantry in the Marines, typically consisting of a team leader, grenadier, rifleman, and automatic rifleman

**flak jacket:** a vest made of bullet-resistant Kevlar and nylon, designed to stop fragments from grenades, rockets, and bullets; also called body armor

**forward operating base (FOB):** a small, secure, sometimes temporary base typically closer to combat situations than the main operating base

**grenadier:** an infantryman equipped with grenades

**grunt:** slang for infantryman

**Gunny:** nickname for gunnery sergeant

**helo:** slang for helicopter

**Humvee:** a wide-bodied, all-terrain four-wheel-drive truck

**IED:** an improvised explosive device typically known as a roadside bomb

**insurgent:** a person who takes part in an armed rebellion; a militant

**IV:** short for intravenous; a fluid drip administered directly into a vein

**kill zone:** an area in a battle where the enemy hopes to kill the most soldiers

**leatherneck:** slang for Marine

**M1A1 Abrams tank:** a well-armed, heavily armored, highly mobile main battle tank

**M4:** a lightweight, short-barreled military assault rifle

**M16:** the most widely used military automatic assault rifle

**M203:** a single-shot grenade launcher that attaches to the M16 or M4 carbine

**M240B:** a standard infantry medium machine gun

**M249:** a light machine gun used as a squad automatic weapon

**magazine:** container holding rounds of ammunition that is inserted into a weapon

**medevac:** a term for medical evacuation; a mission flown by helicopters to remove wounded personnel from a battle area

**militant:** a person who takes part in an armed rebellion; an insurgent

**MK19:** a belt-fed automatic 40-mm grenade launcher

**morphine:** a strong painkiller

**mortar:** a muzzle-loading, high-angle gun with a short barrel that fires shells at high elevations for a short range

**mosque:** a Muslim house of worship

**MP:** military police

**platoon:** a small military unit typically consisting of three squads of between 20 and 30 persons per squad

**Purple Heart:** a U.S. military decoration awarded to members of the armed forces who have been wounded in action

**quick reaction force:** a small military group that is poised to respond on short notice, typically less than 15 minutes, to a combat situation

**recon:** short for doing a reconnaissance, an exploration or examination of an area to gather military information

**RPG:** rocket-propelled grenade launched from a shoulder-fired portable weapon

**RPK:** a hand-held light machine gun, originally manufactured in the former Soviet Union

**SMAW:** shoulder-fired multipurpose assault weapon

**SAW:** a squad automatic weapon, typically an M249 light machine gun

**shrapnel:** fragments from an exploded mine, bomb, or shell

**spider hole:** a well-hidden hole, often connected to others by a tunnel, used to fight from or to escape to

**suppressive fire:** a flurry of rounds directed at the enemy to keep them pinned down and prevent them from shooting at moving targets; also called cover fire

**tour** or **tour of duty:** a period of time spent assigned to service in a foreign country

**tracer round:** a bullet filled with a flare that burns bright, giving the shooter a better aim on a moving target

**turret:** a self-contained weapons platform housing guns on a vehicle and capable of rotation

# About the Author

Allan Zullo is the author of more than ninety nonfiction books on subjects ranging from sports and the supernatural to history and animals.

He has written the bestselling Haunted Kids series, published by Scholastic, which is filled with chilling stories based on, or inspired by, documented cases from the files of ghost hunters. Allan also has introduced Scholastic readers to the Ten True Tales series, gripping stories of extraordinary persons — many of them young people — who have met the challenges of dangerous, sometimes life-threatening, situations. Among the books in the series are *World War II Heroes* and *Teens at War*. In addition, he has authored two books about the real-life experiences of kids during the Holocaust — *Survivors: True Stories of Children in the Holocaust* and *Heroes of the Holocaust: True Stories of Rescues by Teens.*

Allan, the grandfather of four and the father of two grown daughters, lives with his wife, Kathryn, on a mountainside near Asheville, North Carolina. To learn more about the author, visit his Web site at www.allanzullo.com.